Friend of the Artist
Summer 2017

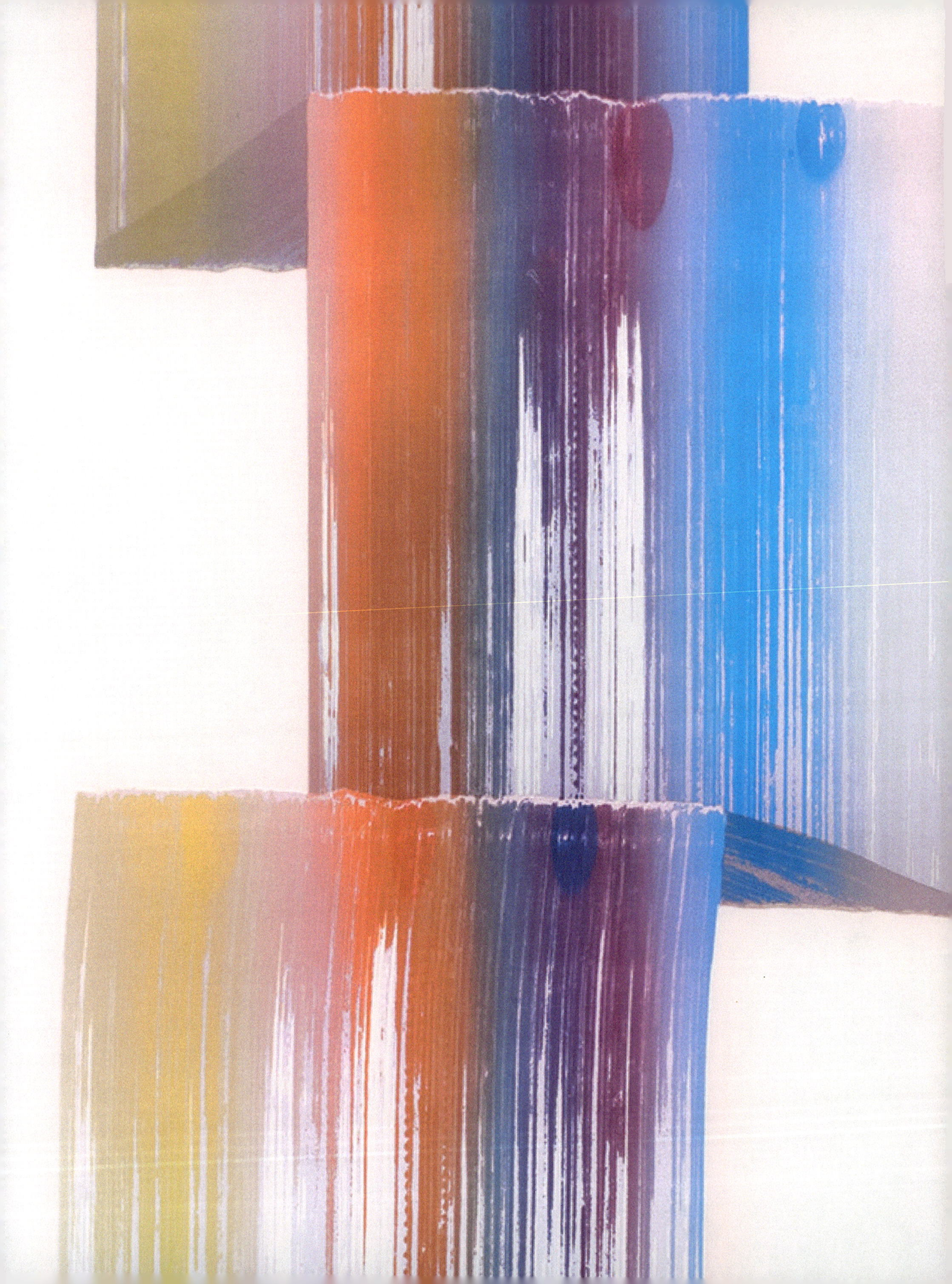

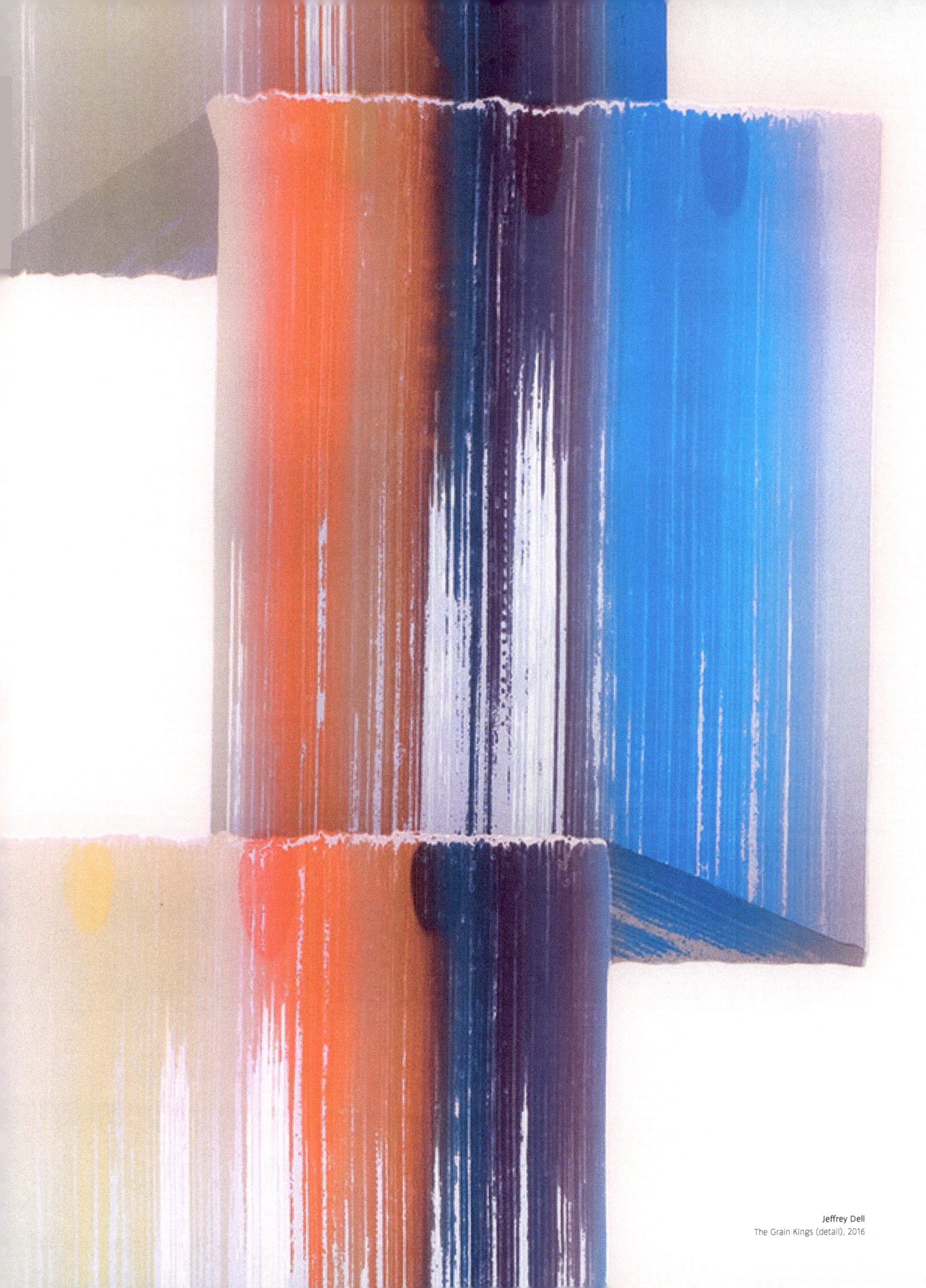

Jeffrey Dell
The Grain Kings (detail), 2016

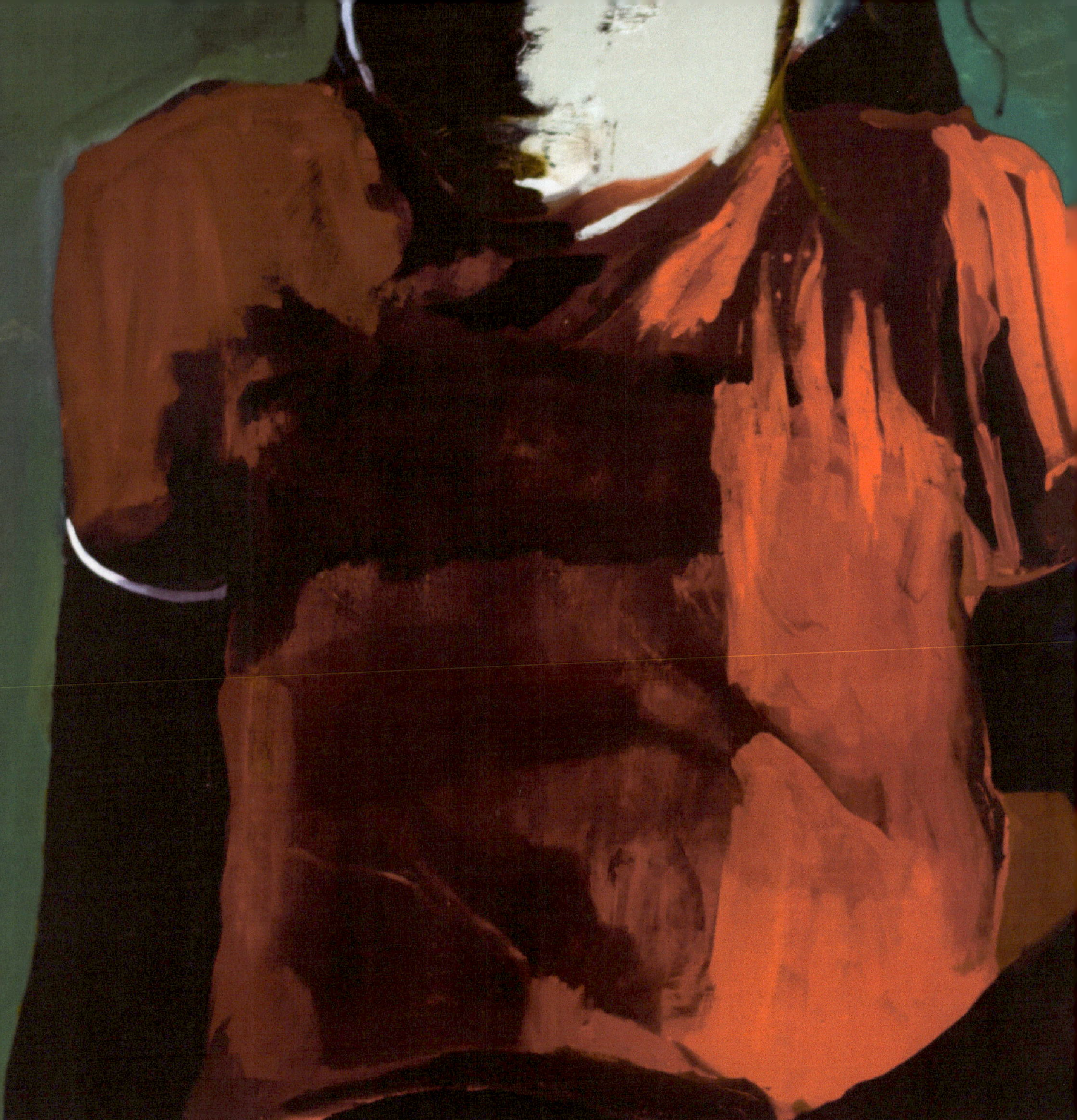

Friend of the Artist (FOA)
friendoftheartist.com
contact@friendoftheartist.com

Produced and printed in the United States of America

Designed by Chase Christensen, chasech.com
Editing by Dannie Liebergot

ISBN: 9780692932131

Ekaterina Vanovskay
Red Sweater, 2017
(detail)

FOUND ON PAGE 87

Contents

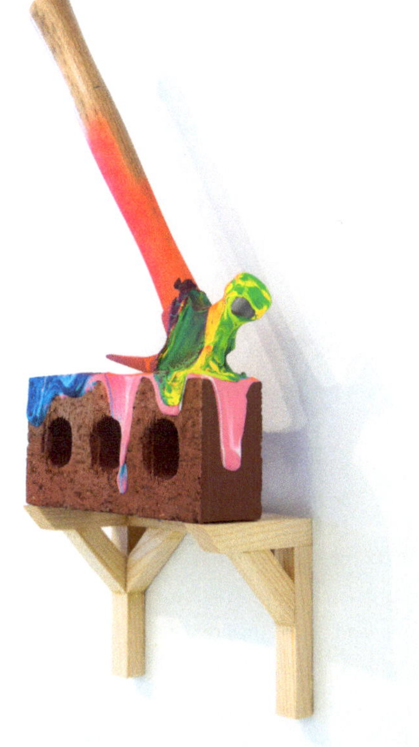

Justin Korver
Relating or the Cliche of a Rock
and a Hard Place, 2017
(detail)

FOUND ON PAGE 61

Opening Remarks

FRIEND OF THE ARTIST exists to showcase the work of talented artists from around the world. There is much engaging artwork out there, but because of an invisible gap between the academy and the art world, there is a limit to the opportunities that artists have. Paintings collect dust and voices become mute. Our print and digital publication allows us to show artist's work in a broader context through our newly designed publication. We have the advantage of engaging in open dialogue with our artist interviews and articles which makes us unique from other art organizations. It's all about the art and creating a meaningful dialogue around it in a printed form.

The submissions for our Summer 2017 issue doubled from our previous publication and includes successful artists that graduated from top art programs such as Yale and SMFA. They represent four different countries and three of the artists in the publication are full-time professors. We got a chance to have a conversation with Hollis Hammonds, who is the Chair of the Visual Arts at St. Edwards University in Austin, Texas. Her work has been shown in museums and galleries across the country. We thoroughly enjoyed speaking to her are thrilled to share our conversation with you. In addition to this conversation, we also interviewed Texas photographer, Peter Hiatt, and New York based performance artist, Bonam Kim.

In this issue, we focused on selecting work that contributes to the conversation about art in the art world. We partnered with curator Samantha Keith, of Fresh Contemporary, to talk about the work of four artists. We appreciate the insight she brings to the work and hope you enjoy this new section. This is the first issue where we partnered with another art organization, and we look forward to working with others in the future. Also, special thanks to Chase Christensen who redesigned the publication from the ground up. TY BISHOP, *Publisher*

When I sat down to jury the Summer 2017 artist submissions with Ty and Dannie I was truly excited. Over the last few publications we have had several talented artists from different states and countries around the world. Each publication has grown since FOA was created, and it is my dream that it will continue to do so for the service of artists worldwide. Yet, with the Summer Publication there was something unique. For the past year we have primarily had 2-D artists applying, with the occasional sculpture. We received several 3-D works, ranging from ready-mades, to installations, to performance based works. In the Summer 2017 publication you will see a range of ways to engage with the artists, from their images and personal statements, to interviews and essays. To all the artists who applied, thank you. We look forward to continuing to create content, and to truly be a Friend of the Artist.

JUSTIN ARCHER, *Communications Manager*

Summer 2017 highlights Friend of the Artist's progress and achievements thus far as a new art publication. Many national and international artists submitted to our Summer 2017 issue, and we are incredibly thankful for their efforts, support, and engagement with the art community. Selecting the work was challenging and rewarding as we found ourselves participating in the conversation as facilitators, jurors, and fellow artists. The work is bold, powerful, and influential and flows eloquently throughout the magazine. We at FOA are delighted to share the selected artists and their hard work. As always, we are here to provide opportunities for artists and to have a conversation on all things art. Enjoy!

DANNIE LIEBERGOT, *Media Manager & Editor*

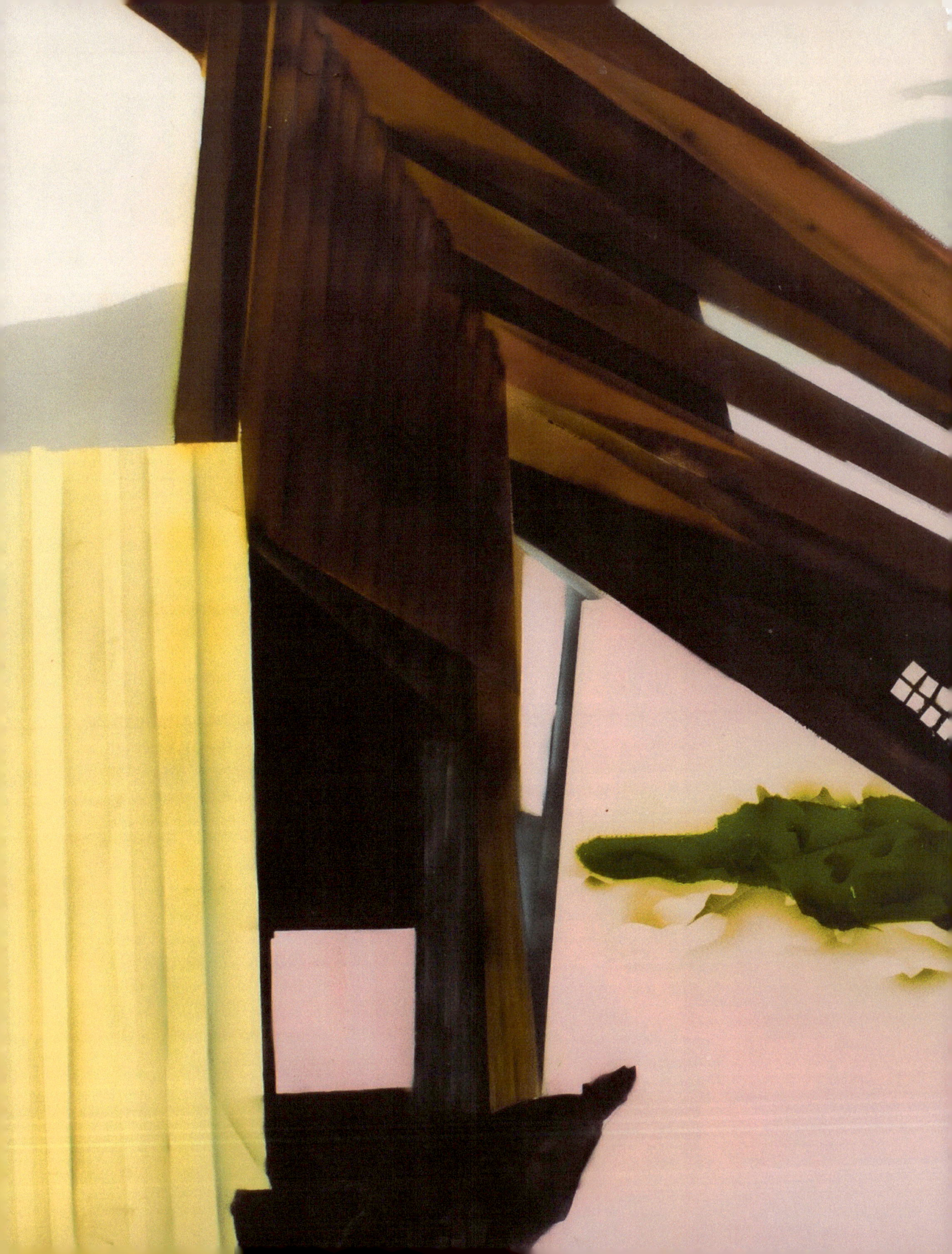

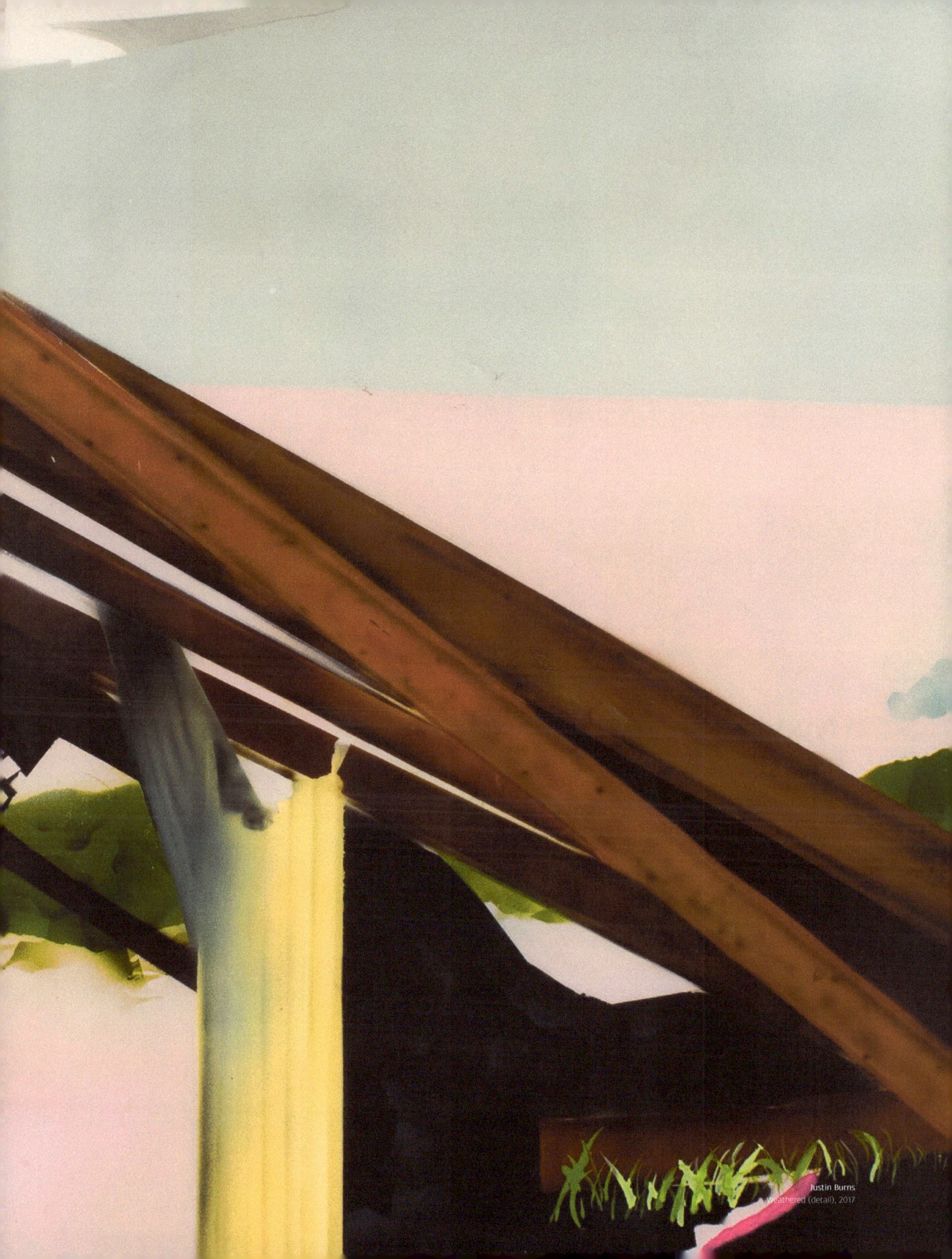

Justin Burns
Weathered (detail), 2017

Hyun Jung Ahn *Brooklyn, New York* hyunjungahn.com

I speak in a private, furtive pictograph. It is indirect speech through enigmatic abstract shapes. The shapes are capsules of time, feelings and words, which I cannot express verbally. They pile up in me and I collect them. They combine and crystallize. The different shapes suggest emotions and states of being. As a collection, the compositions have a conversational relationship with each other and create narratives. I begin with drawing in my visual diary. Then, I create drawings and paintings and wooden sculptures based on the shapes in the diary. I show the natural surface of my materials (Unprimed canvas, rough-edged paper, and wood) as much as I can. The revealed material looks vulnerable like the naked body; It exposes my naked mind. After I moved to New York, The language barrier allowed me to choose an alternate way to express myself. I am exploring my own voice and developing an ability to speak in this process.

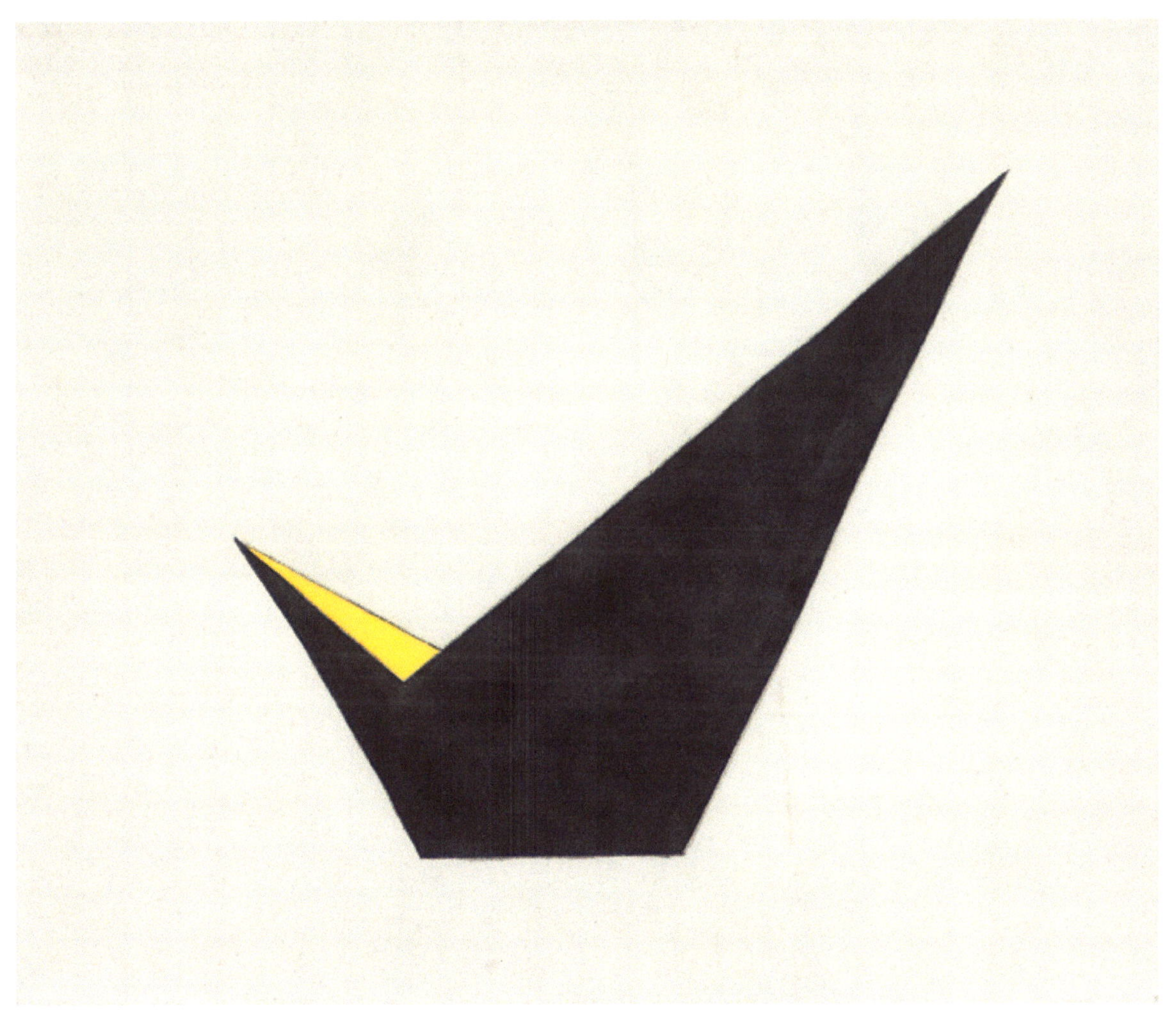

Hyan Jung Ahn
I'll Rock You, 2017
Acrylic on canvas,
20 x 24 in.

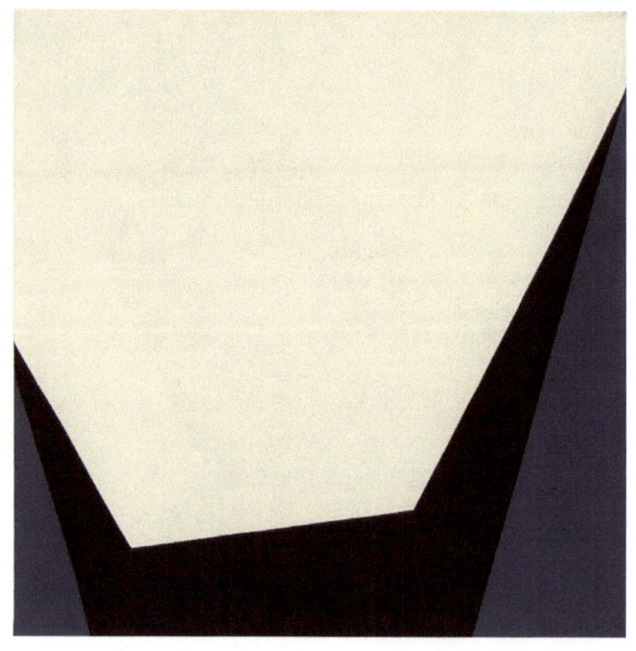

Hyan Jung Ahn
My Favorites Series, 2016
Acrylic on canvas,
20 x 20 in.
20 x 20 in.

Hyan Jung Ahn
Night Air, 2016
Acrylic on canvas,
24 x 24 in.
24 x 24in.

Sirimas Benz Amatayakul

Chicago, Illinois   amatayastudio.com

I paint almost exclusively with my two children (4 and 6 years old). They introduced me to process-based painting and gave me the courage to finally start my own artist journey at age 34. They still allow me to paint alongside them and eagerly jump in when I ask for help.

My process honors the rawness, innocence, courage, joy, and spontaneity that I found in my children's art-making process. My paintings are simply my spontaneous and unfiltered responses to my creative urges. My process is straightforward. I don't plan ahead on how I want my paintings to look. I follow my impulses, choose colors and make marks that feel right to me at the time.

My highest hope is to make approachable, open-ended and inviting art that inspires other reluctant painters (or artists, or anyone) to try their hands at art without being too hard on themselves.

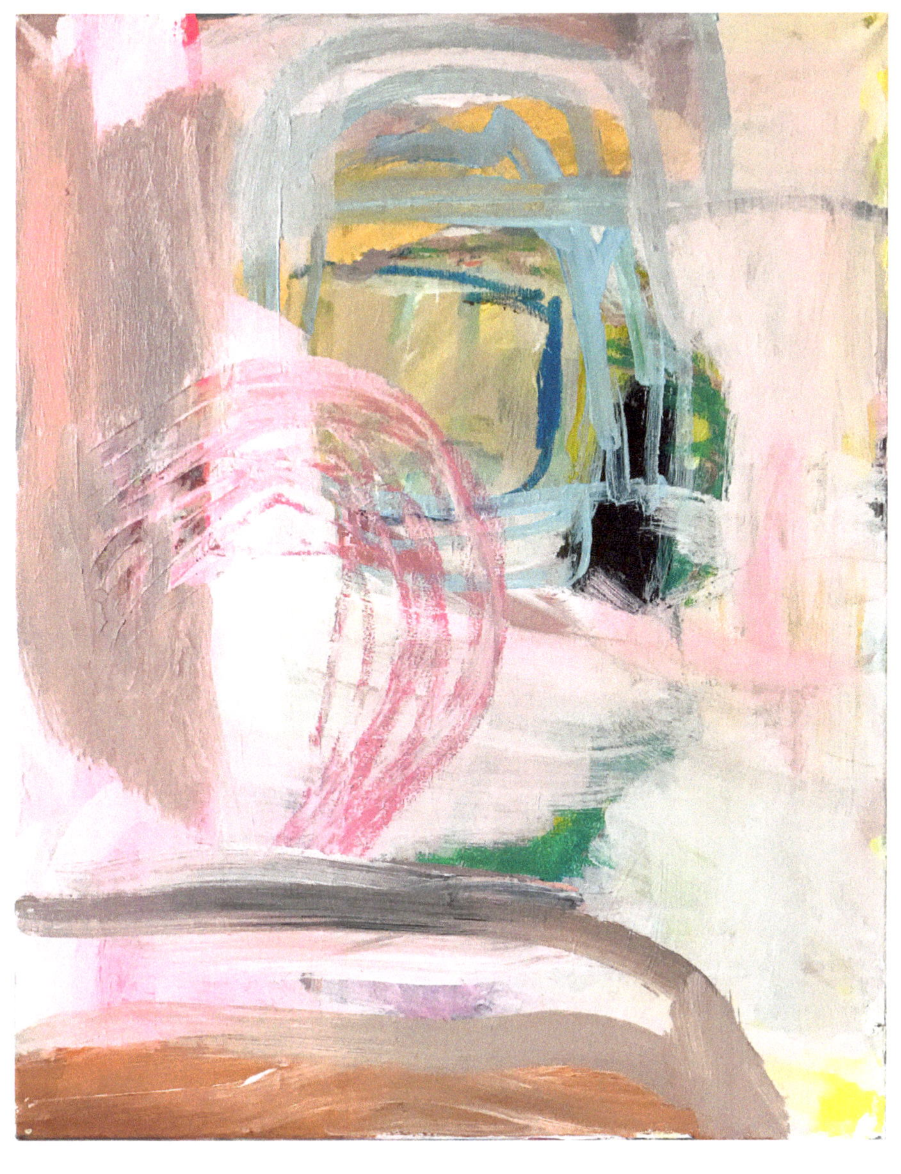

Sirimas Benz Amatayakul
Because Why Not, 2017
Acrylic and oil pastel on canvas,
12 x 16 in.

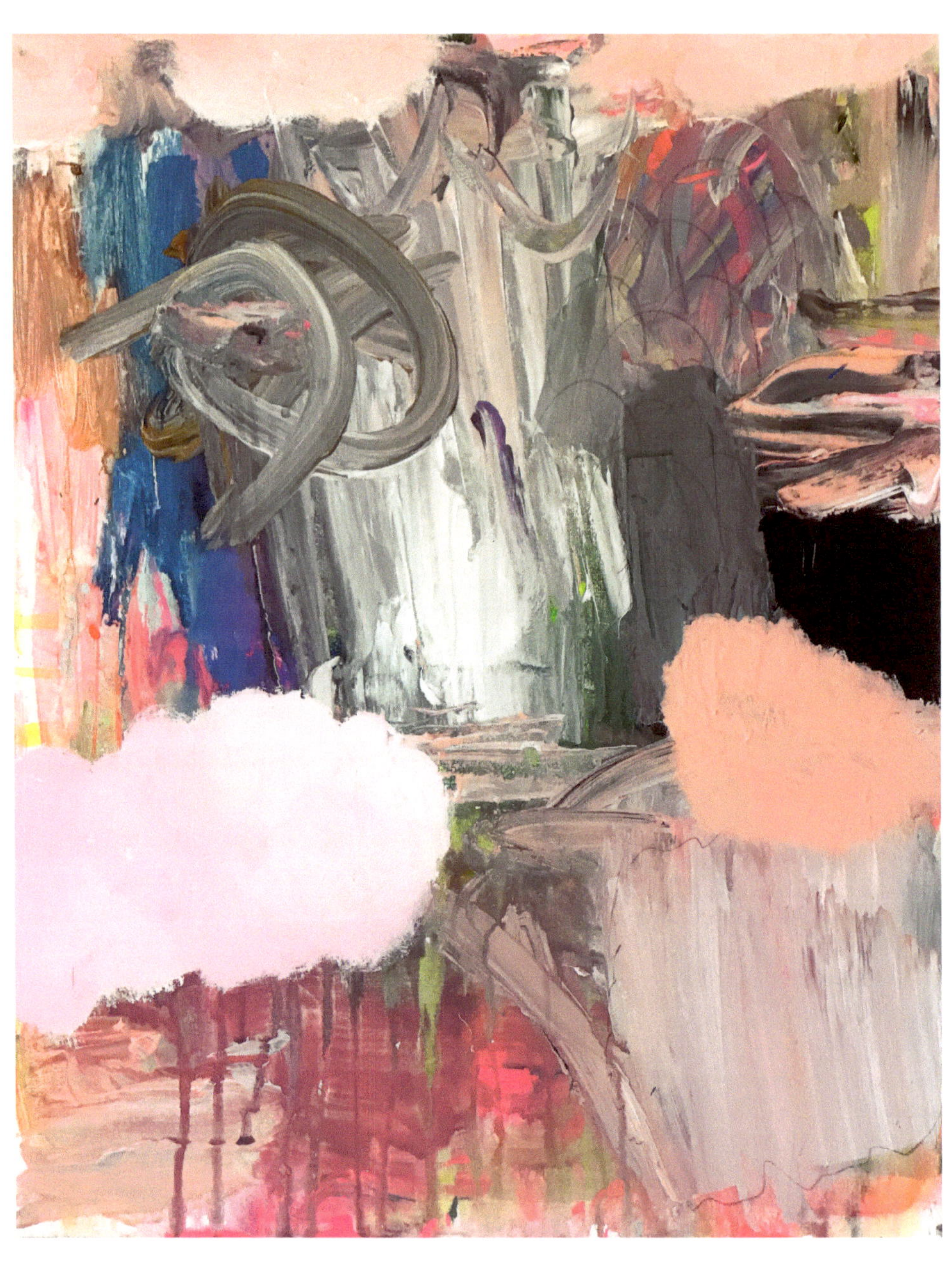

Sirimas Benz Amatayakul
Creative Debut 2, 2017
Acrylic and oil pastel on canvas.
12 x 16 in.

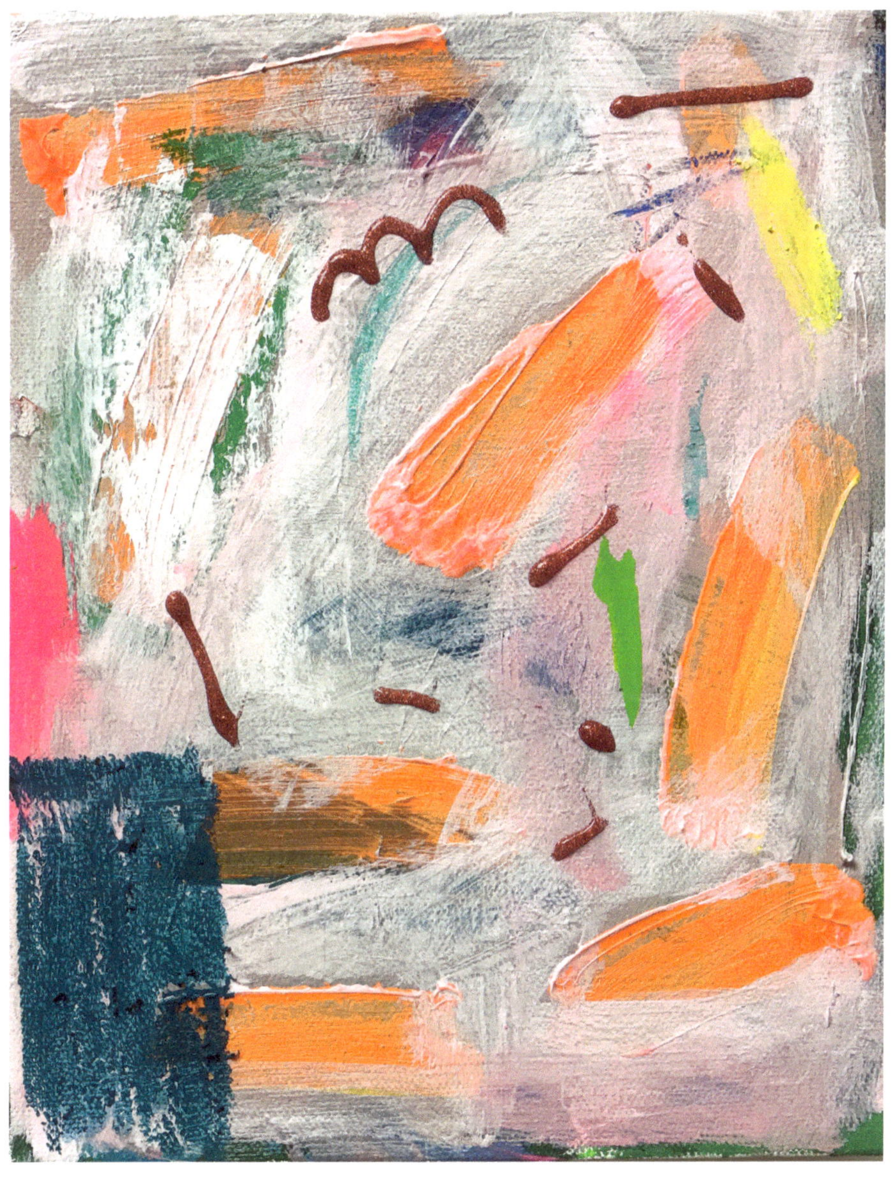

Sirimas Benz Amatayakul
I'm Pretty Good at Messy 2, 2017
Acrcylic, oil pastel, glitter glue on canvas,
8 x 10 in.

Miya Ando

Long Island, New York   miyaando.com

Miya Ando is an American artist whose metal canvases and sculpture articulate themes of perception and ones relationship to time. Half Japanese & half Russian-American, Ando is a descendant of Bizen sword makers and spent part of her childhood in a Buddhist temple in Japan as well as on 25 acres of redwood forest in rural coastal Northern California. She has continued her 16th generation Japanese sword smithing and Buddhist lineage by combining metals, reflectivity and light in her luminous paintings and sculpture.

Living in the rural wilderness of California instilled an awareness and attention to nature and natural materials. This love of elements and natural phenomena was further refined while living in Japan. The foundation of Ando's practice has been the transformation and combining of natural elements and utilization of the vernacular of nature. She utilizes vocabulary drawn from the natural world to investigate perception and ones relationship to time. Her focus has been on the transformation of surfaces and the use of elemental materials to create shifting, mutable objects and experiences that change depending upon the light or time of day or viewer's perspective. Her interest is in creating artworks that allow viewers to experience a relationship to nature and to truly be in the moment as they encounter the transitory qualities of light. Her hope is to draw people into a slowed-down environment with artwork that is experiential and employs the visual vocabulary of natural phenomena and transformation. She utilizes contemporary forms and techniques as well as industrial materials as an examination and harmonizing of the man-made and the natural.

In 2011 she completed two memorial sculptures for 9/11 in which she utilized 30 foot tall pieces of steel that had fallen from the World Trade Center Buildings. CONTINUED ON PAGE 94 →

Miya Ando
Kumo (Cloud), 2016
Ink and oil on stainless composite,
48 x 48 in.

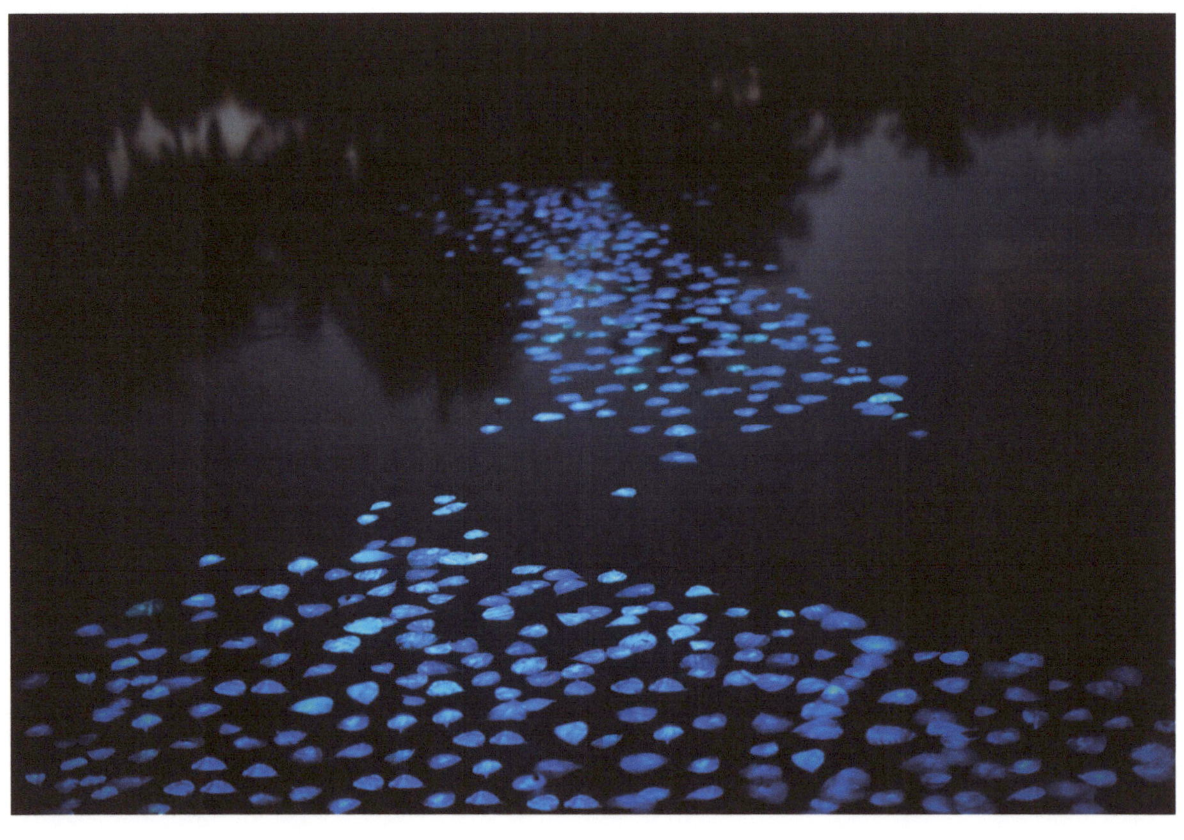

Miya Ando
Obon (The returning of
the spirits), 2012–ongoing
Skeleton leaves, phosphorescence, resin,
1200 x 1200 in. (variable)

Miya Ando
Yugen (The mystery of nature), 2017
pigment, urethane, resin,
dye on aluminum,
36 x 36 in.

Justin Burns

Fort Worth, Texas   justinlburns.net

My work deals with the decaying era of a small Texas town where all that is left is the memory of how things used to be. I begin photographing interiors and the outside of weathered relic structures, that once were an icon, are now headstones. Eventually, these spaces will disappear just like the people who hold special memories to them. I airbrush on multiple transparent layers to emphasize the depth and detail of the space, while also incorporating my own romanticized perception.

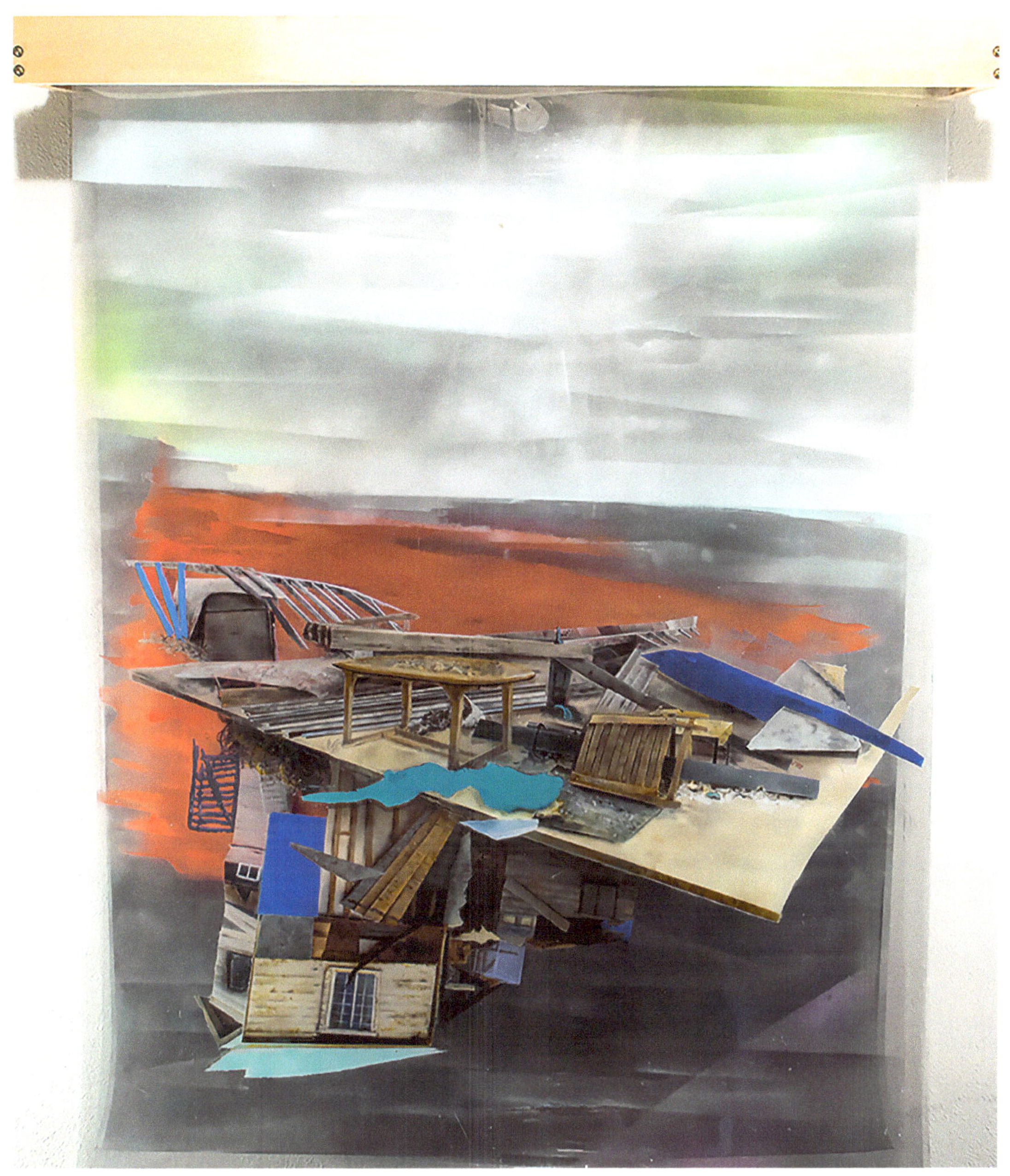

Justin Burns
Just Won't Let It Go, 2017
Airbrush and acrylic on multi-layered duralar,
12 x 12in.

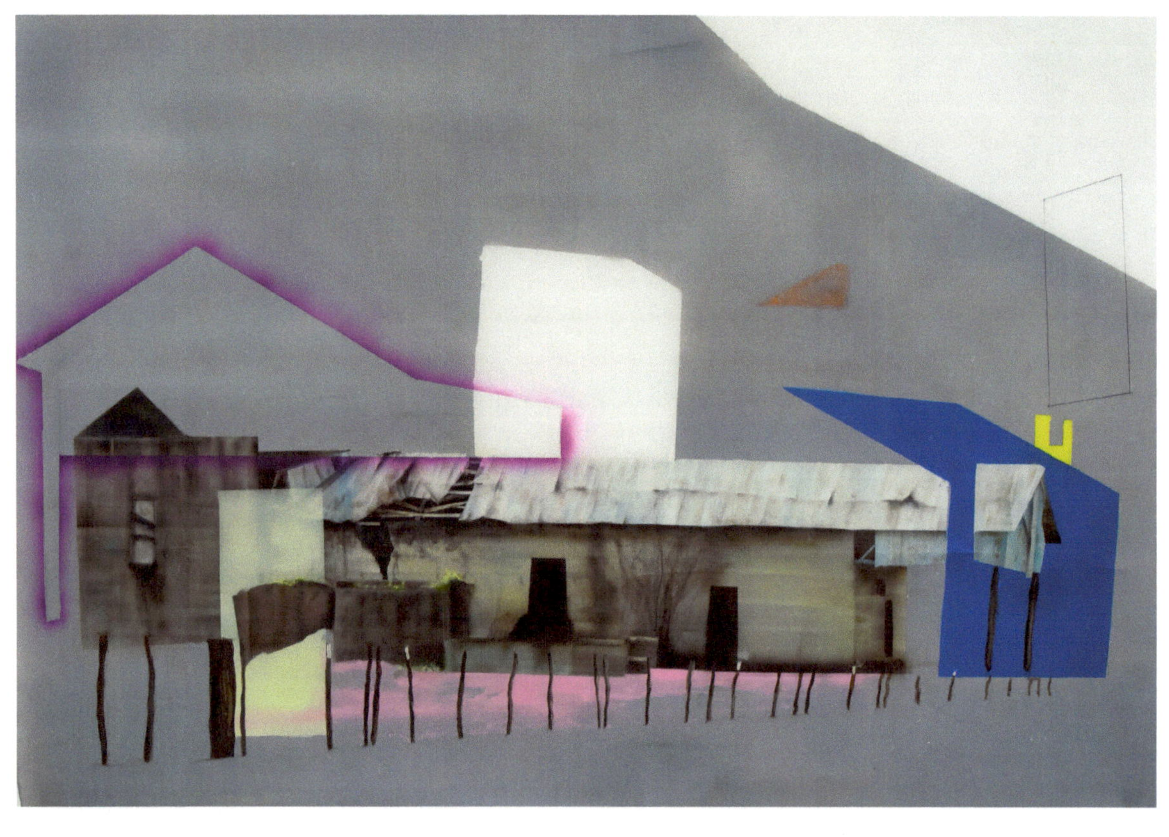

Justin Burns
Since It Closed Down, 2017
Airbrush and acrylic on matte duralar,
31 x 40 in.

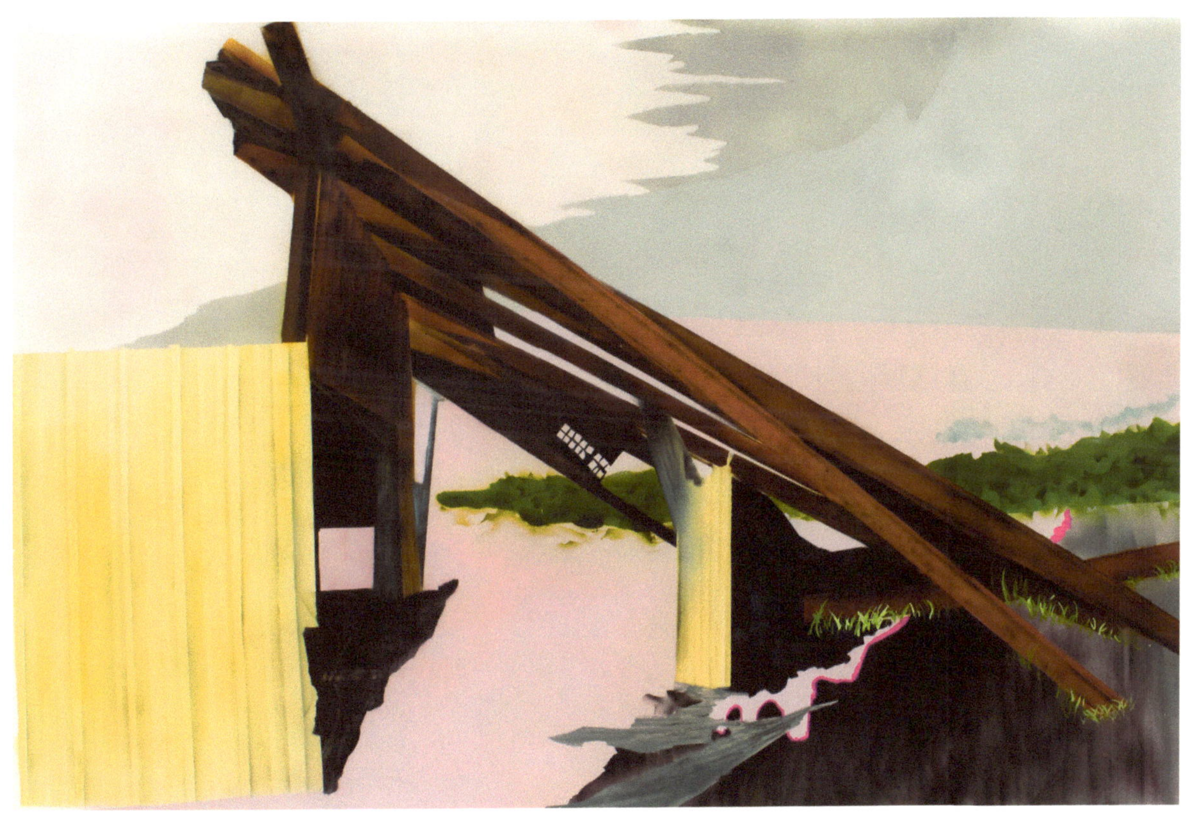

Justin Burns
Weathered, 2017
Airbrush and acrylic on matte duralar,
24 x 45 in.

Lauren Christlieb *Houston, Texas* laurenchristlieb.com

I'm interested in an object's power to create, replace and spark memory. To materialize these thoughts, I documented and then recreated objects from the home left behind by my grandfather. He lived in this home for six years with his mother, before she passed away, and just as my grandfather had done, I went through their quiet rooms and decided what things I would keep, what things I would re-sculpt, what things I would re-print, what things I would re-photograph, and re-bake. These decisions were made intuitively, based on sentiment, and curiosity.

The objects I chose to keep hold historical links to family members and I keep them as reminders and connections. The recreation process allows me the chance to continue spending time with those who possessed the objects before me. It is as if these objects hold some untold truth or power and spending time with them would somehow reveal something to me. Each of these objects is a part of my family's shared history, and thus it is through these things that I reconnect with the past and create new connections in the present.

For example, my grandfather constantly raved about a chocolate iced box cake that his mother used to make. When he passed away I found all of her recipes. There were stacks of them. But for some reason, the chocolate iced box cake recipe was incomplete. I couldn't make the cake, so I decided to recreate the recipe as a three-color silkscreen instead–twice the size of the original. It needed a recipe box twice the size of the original, so I made one out of wood, with details of the original box screen-printed onto it.

CONTINUED ON PAGE 94 →

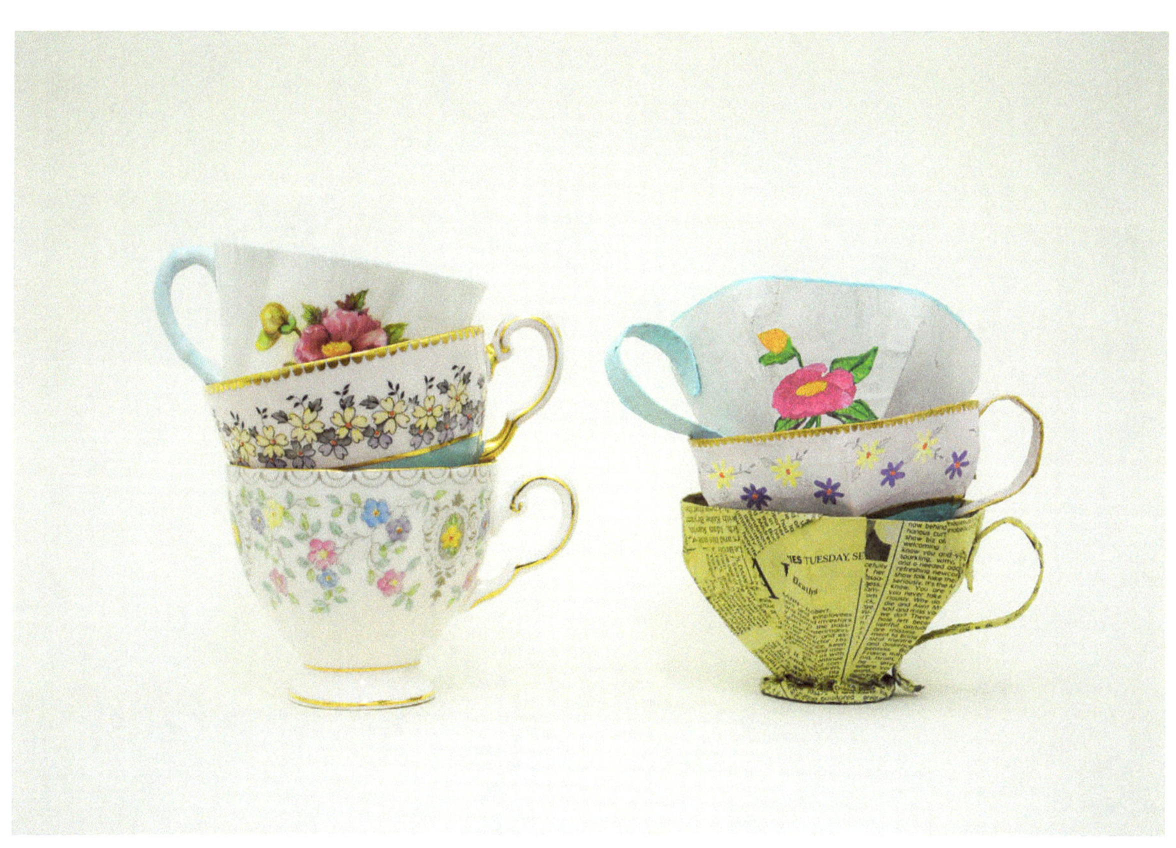

Lauren Christlieb
Because We Never Used Them, 2017
Porcelain, Papier-mâché with obituaries, acrylic

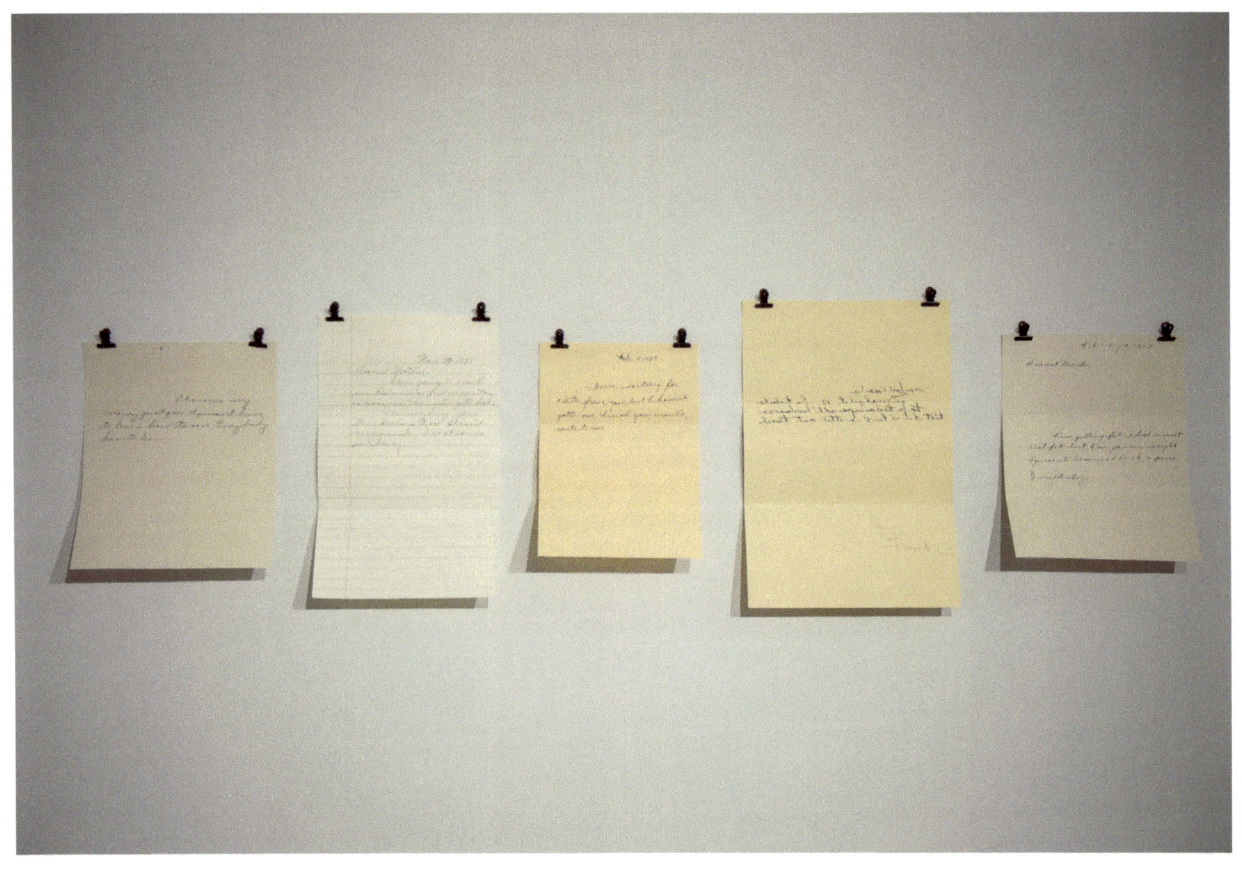

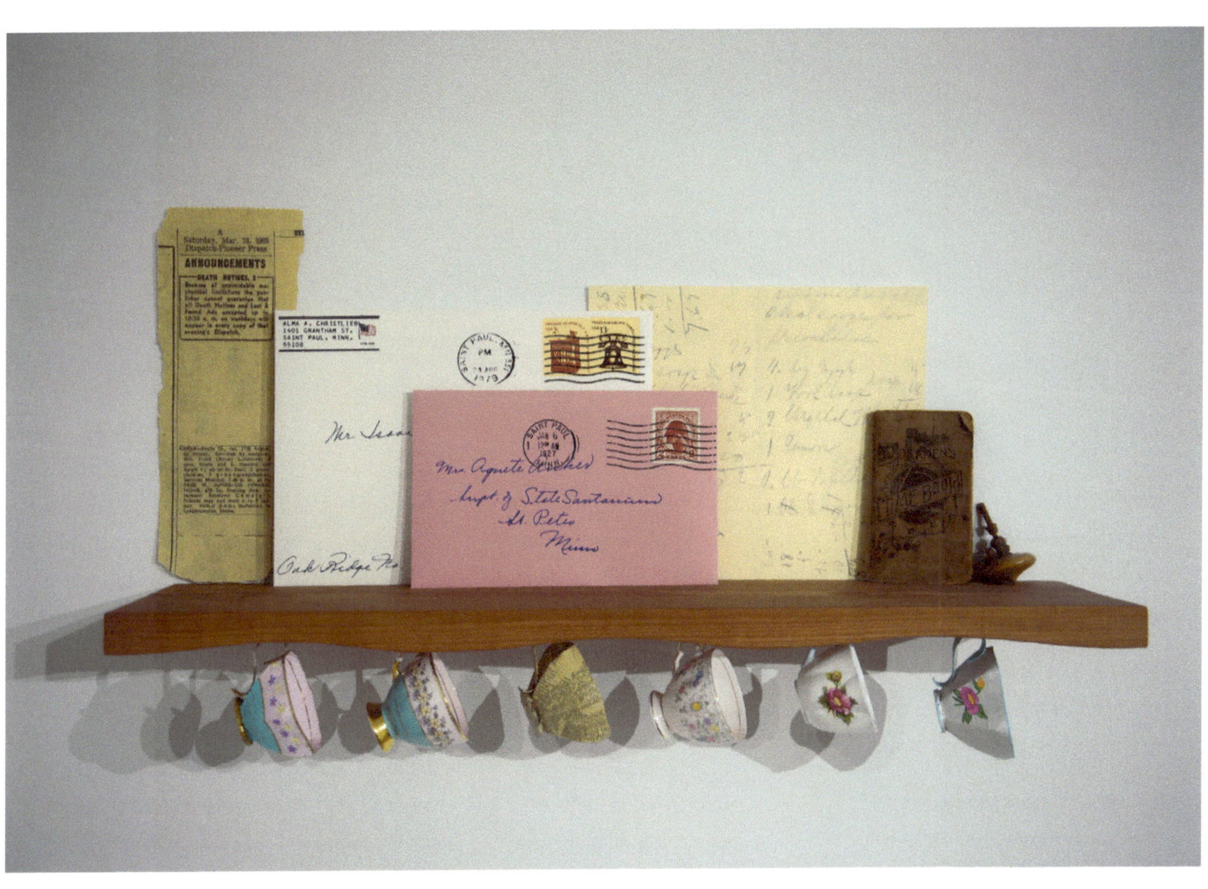

Megan St.Clair   *Los Angeles, California*   meganstclair.com

Emotional identities and intimate awareness are things that fascinate me. Although these conditions cannot be clearly defined, I enjoy the struggle of attempting to examine them or create new questions asking what we think we know about ourselves.

My goal is to question these complicated qualities of closeness through actions, video, metaphor, or object. I expose constructs of identity in the singular self and within the plural unit of a relationship.

Through the reverse engineering of my own memory and experience, I attempt to understand relationships, love, time, vulnerability, and closeness. I do this by becoming transfixed upon my own memories of growing up and discovering the intense ups and downs of emotional vulnerability and honing in on an aspect of it that I can't shake. I am searching for answers about qualities of relationships and what these qualities do for us after a long personal history of failed and abusive past relationships.

I see myself collecting both the positive and negative qualities to use as tools for interpretation in regard to the work. This work is then emerged through the material or the concept of the piece at hand.

These drawings and marks created are not erased nor are they perfected, but are instead they are allowed to exist in their most earnest and imperfect state. This same existence of earnestness in regard to the material is how I feel when reaching back into my own mind for memory of who I am and what I remember about myself at different points in time. The watercolor acts as an atmosphere of memory and a fluid state of searching while the drawings anchor themselves as the people that have shaped my existence and understanding of my own identity.

CONTINUED ON PAGE 95 →

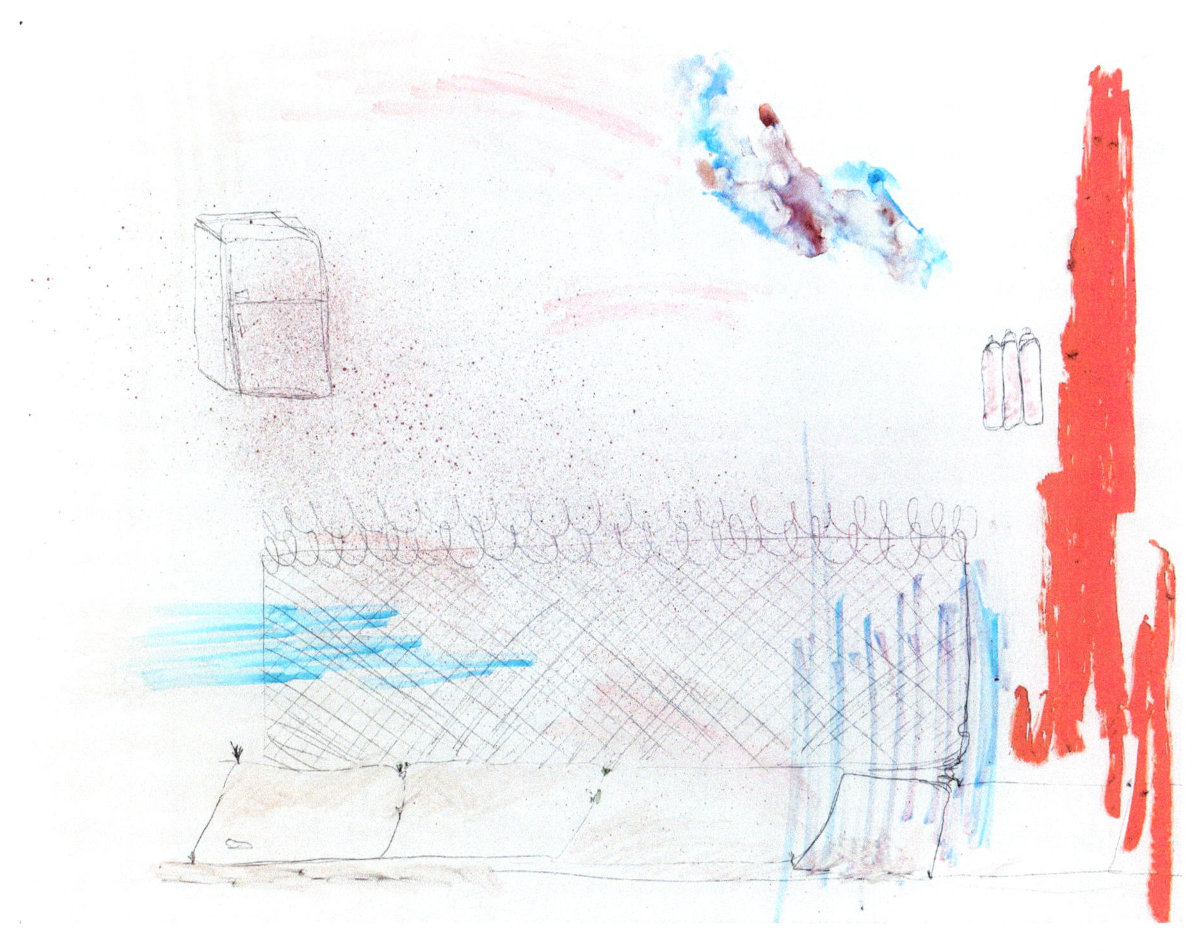

Megan St. Clair
Backhouse, 2017
Spray paint and oil on panel,
18 x 24 in.

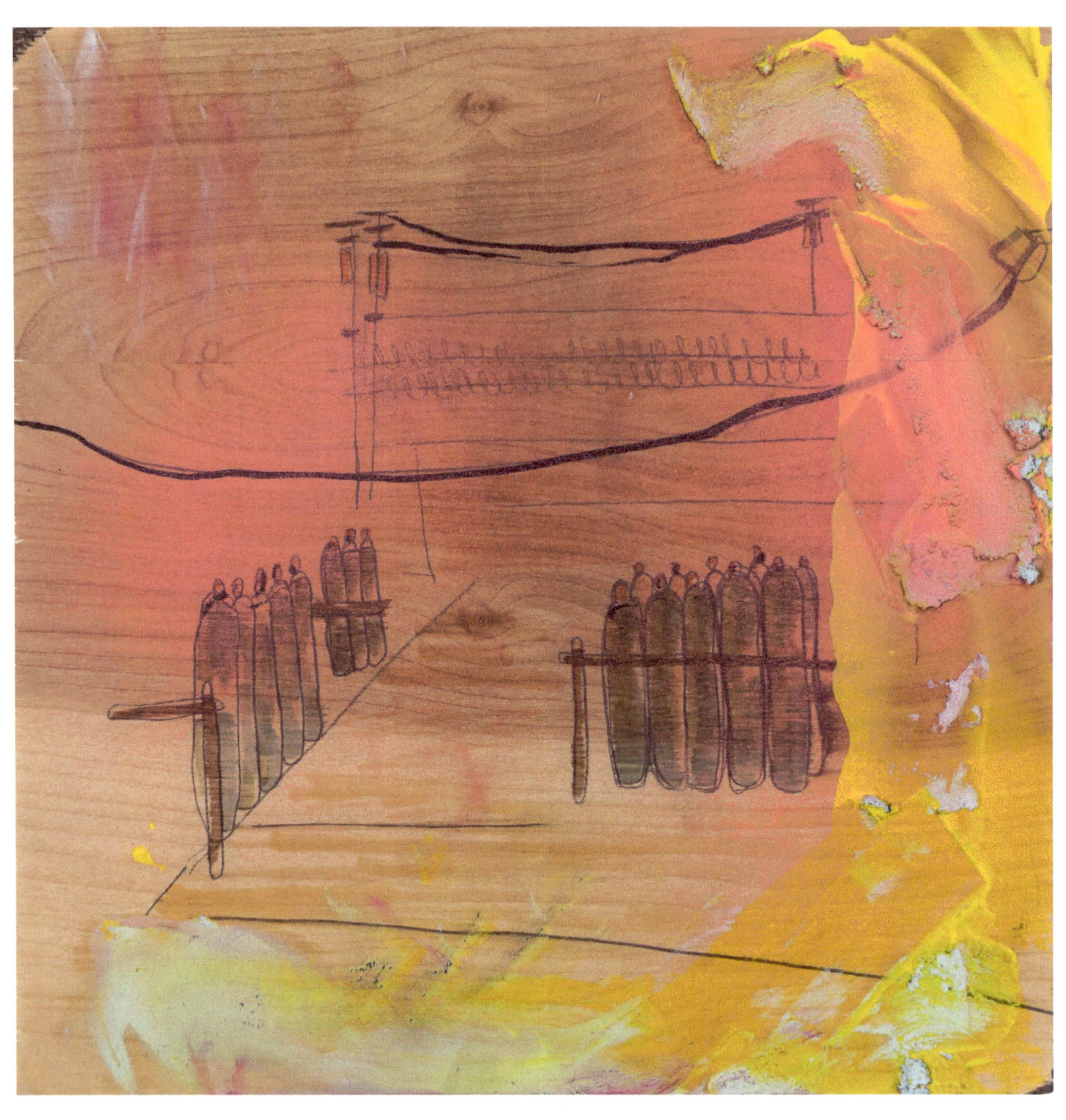

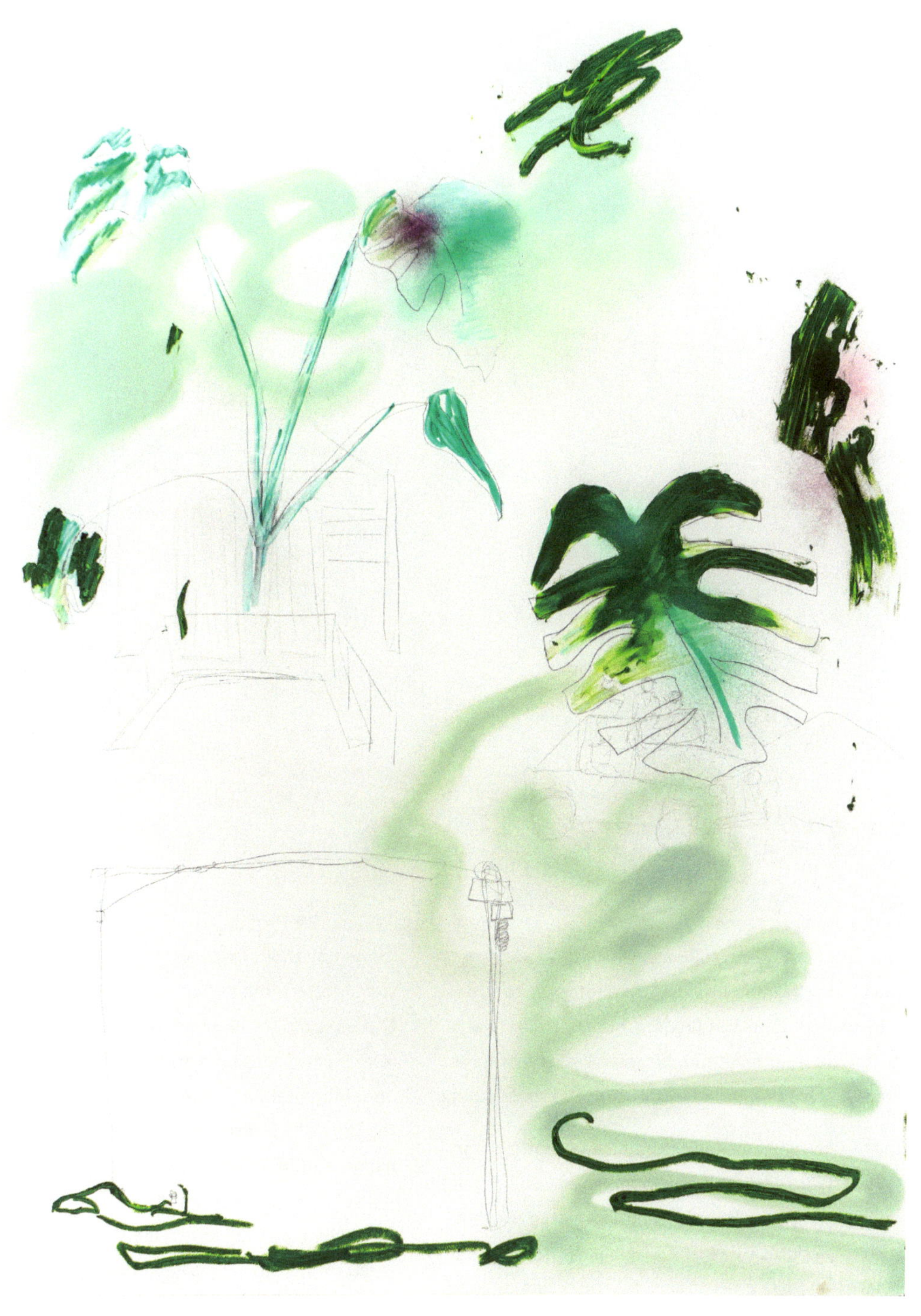

Jeffrey Dell   *San Marcos, Texas*   jeffreydell.com

My recent work contrasts soft, saturated color against near colorlessness, making the work both highly graphic and quietly photographic. The imagery is deceptively neutral: sheets of floating, curled, stacked, and folded paper, or similar forms articulated with brushstrokes. My intent is partly to depict a sense of space that is both convincing and supernatural.

The imagery's simplicity helps us see easily and clearly, but it's also deceptive; colors shift and flux, and our precise perceptual abilities are called into question. I am trying to make an image that is seductive, but where the very thing that seduces us also deceives. Each image is a bit of a promise, a gift that never quite gives. I think it is the nature of visual pleasure to be anticipatory rather than immediate; gazing at an image of cake is not the same as eating it. In bathing my forms in the "magic hour" of twilight, I want to play with this human longing for a time, a place, and a pleasure beyond our reach.

My work regularly references both "high" and "low." My intent is to admit these very human longings, while also acknowledging our folly in projecting desires, and in how much our own perception of the world around us is formed by those longings. My recent titles are stolen from science-fiction novels for which Chris Foss did the cover art. Previous titling came from euphemisms for Area 51 (itself a locus of imagined plots and conspiracies), as well as the titles of a British filmmaker and writer who happens to have had the same name as myself. When I Google myself and these stolen titles, a gloriously confusing mix of the two Jeffrey Dells is returned, both his movies, books and my visual work.

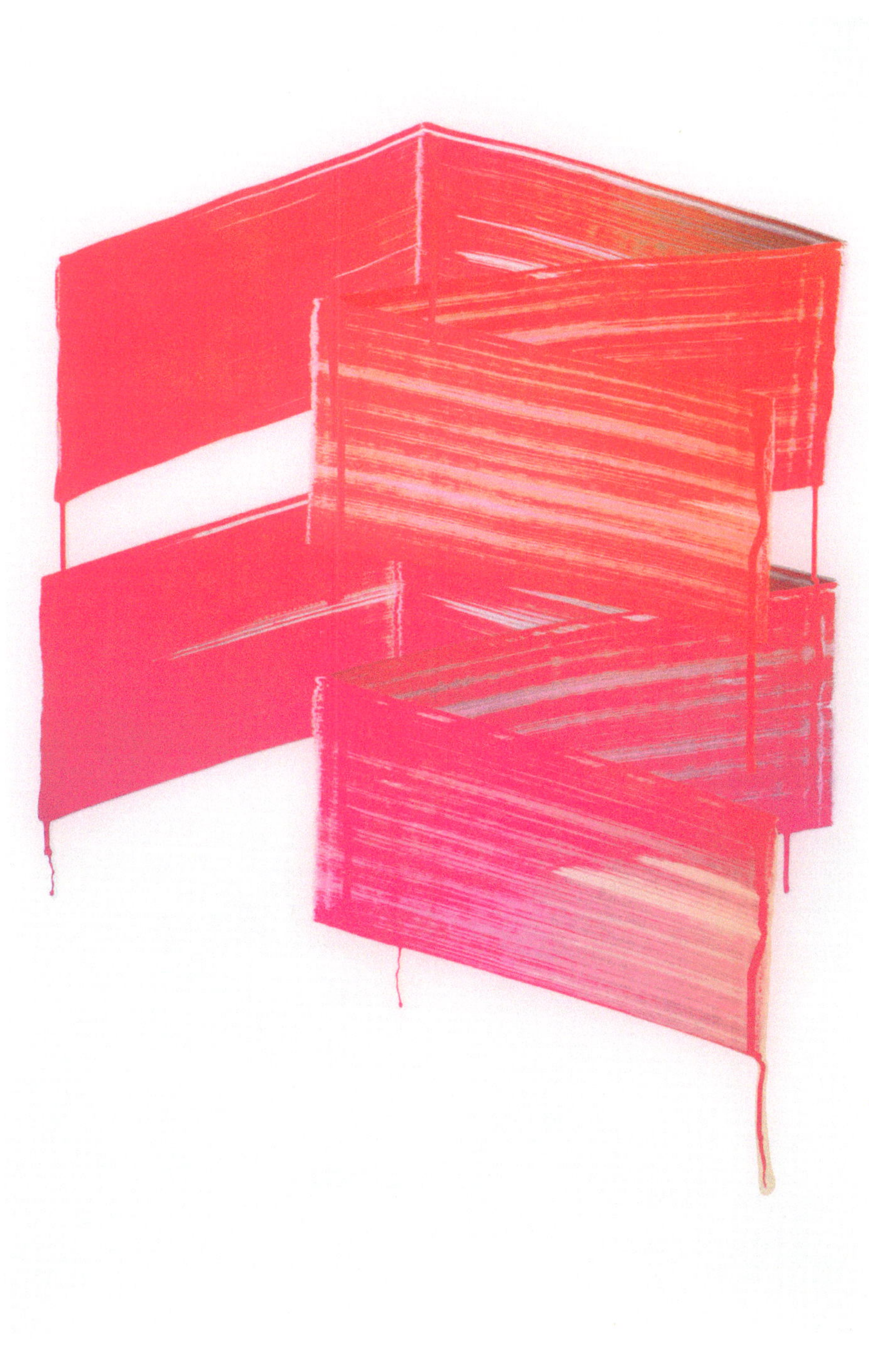

Jeffrey Dell
Second Moonbeast, 2016
Screen print,
34 x 23 in.

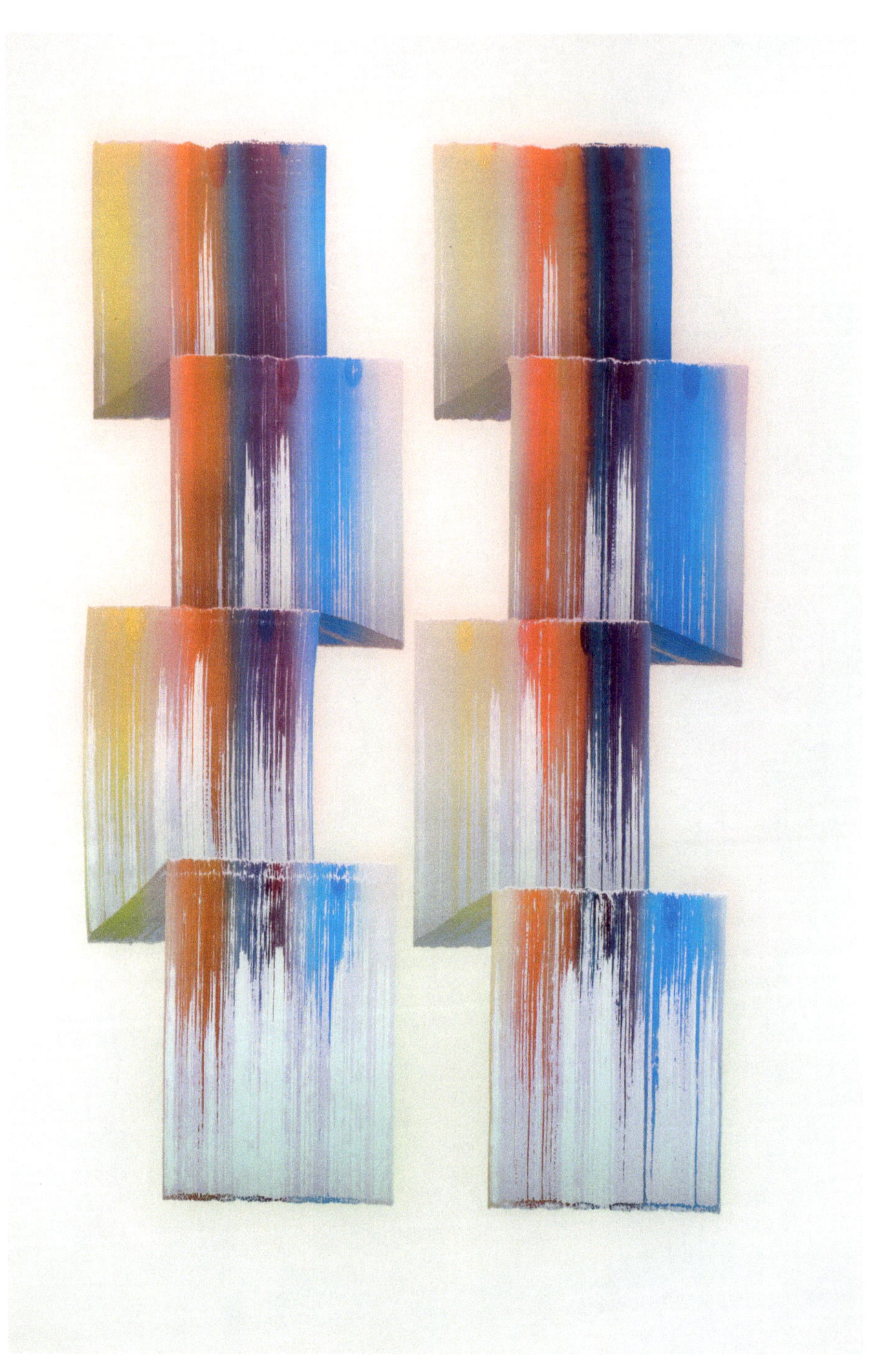

Jeffrey Dell
The Grain Kings, 2016
Screen print,
34 x 23 in.

Friend of The Artist

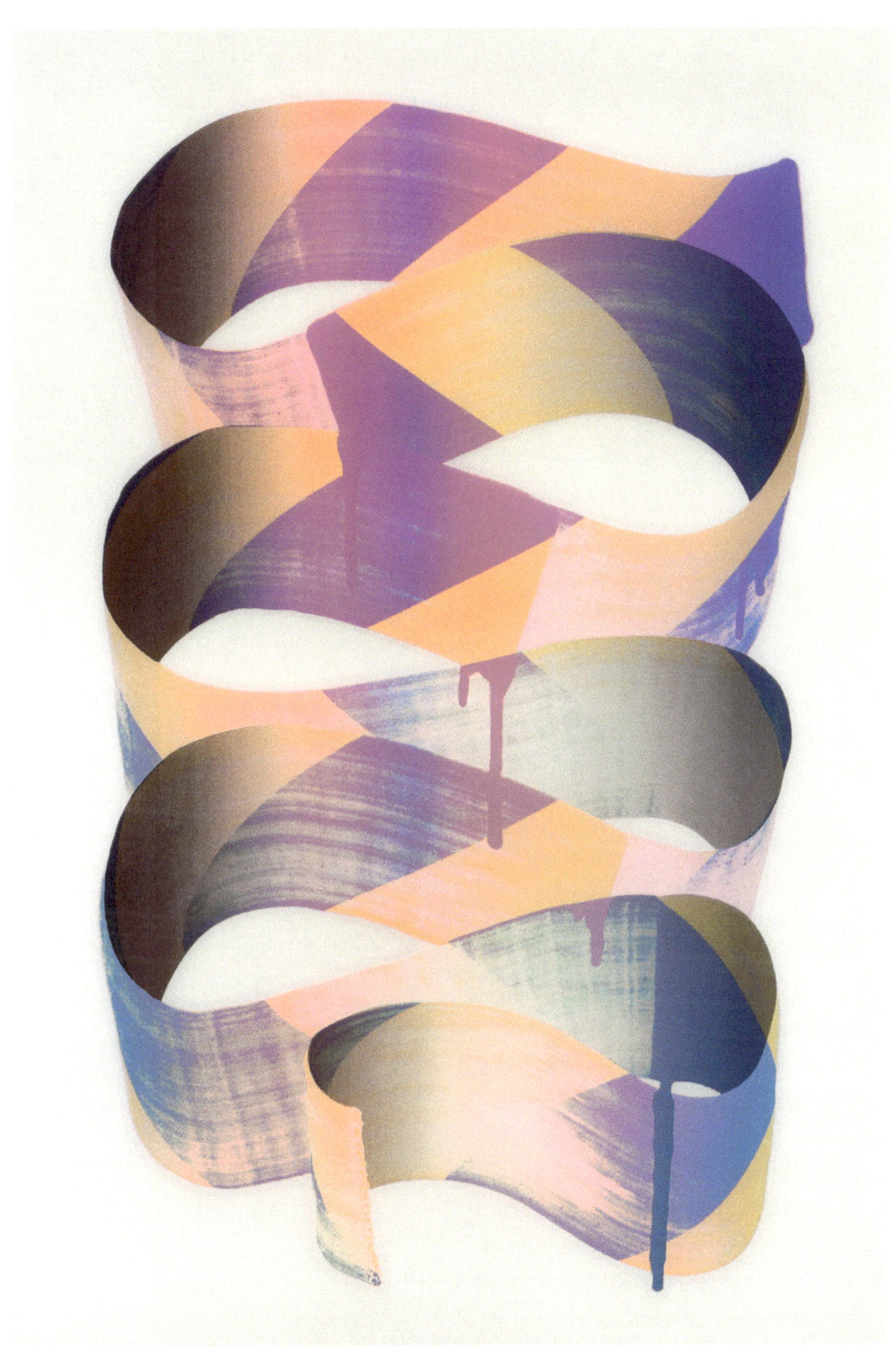

Jeffrey Dell
The Shall Have Stars, 2017
Screen print,
34 x 23 in.

Hollis Hammonds *Austin, Texas* hollishammonds.com

My works are built on threads of personal memory, tied to the public collective consciousness. Evidence of war, injustice, environmental degradation, and consumerist culture are the subjects most often rendered, but the medium itself is as much content as it is form. Whether through drawing or found object sculptures, multiples, collecting, and excess are often important aspects of my work. I'm attempting to illustrate or capture moments in time. Some are re-presentations of the past, others a projection of one potential dystopian future, and others completely from the realm of fantasy. Interested in how these worlds of truth and fiction as well as past and future both intersect and overlap, I develop narrative representations that play on these dualities. For me, drawing is an important ritualistic activity, imbuing meaning onto representations of events and superficial objects, making them more precious in some way.

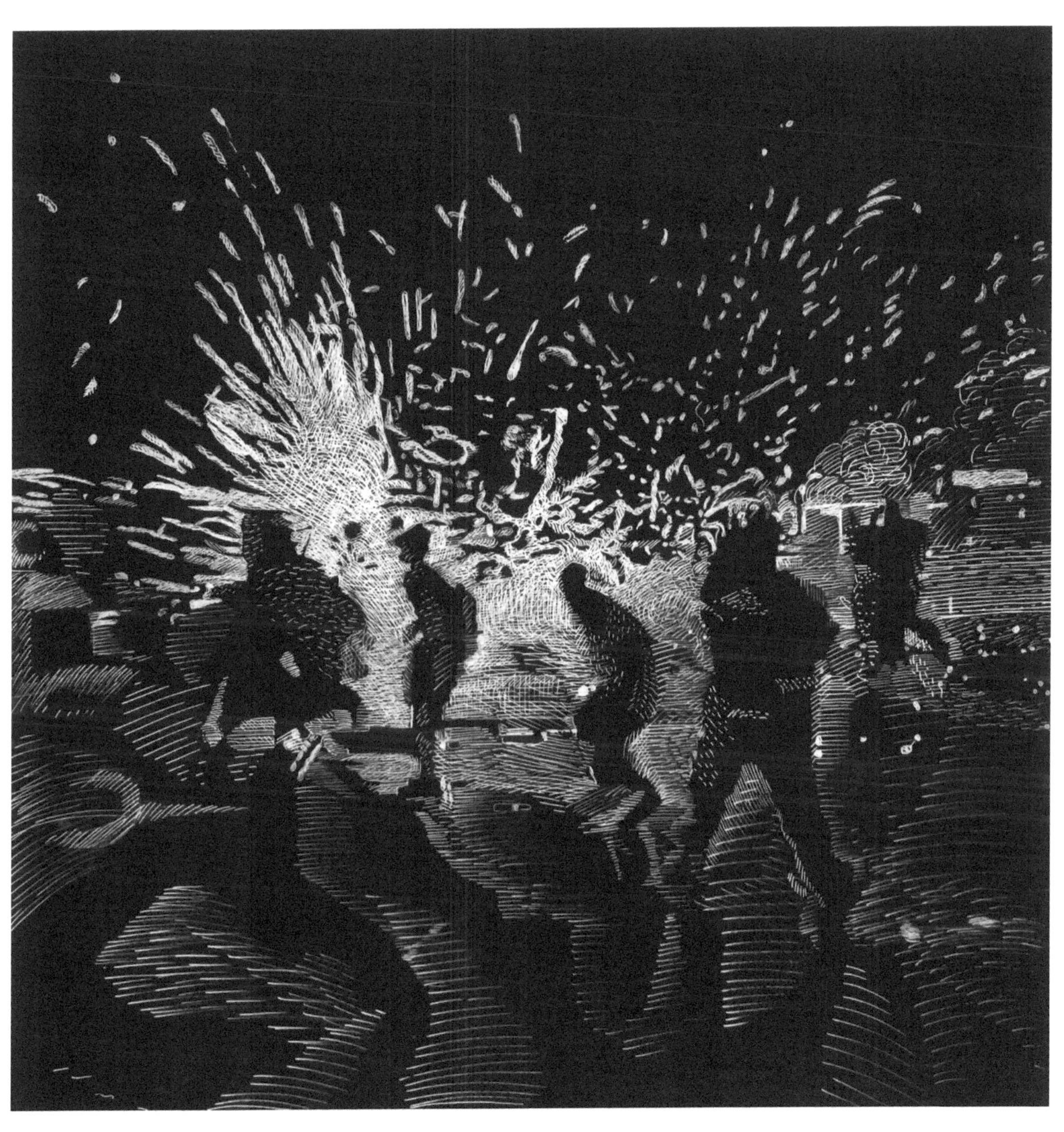

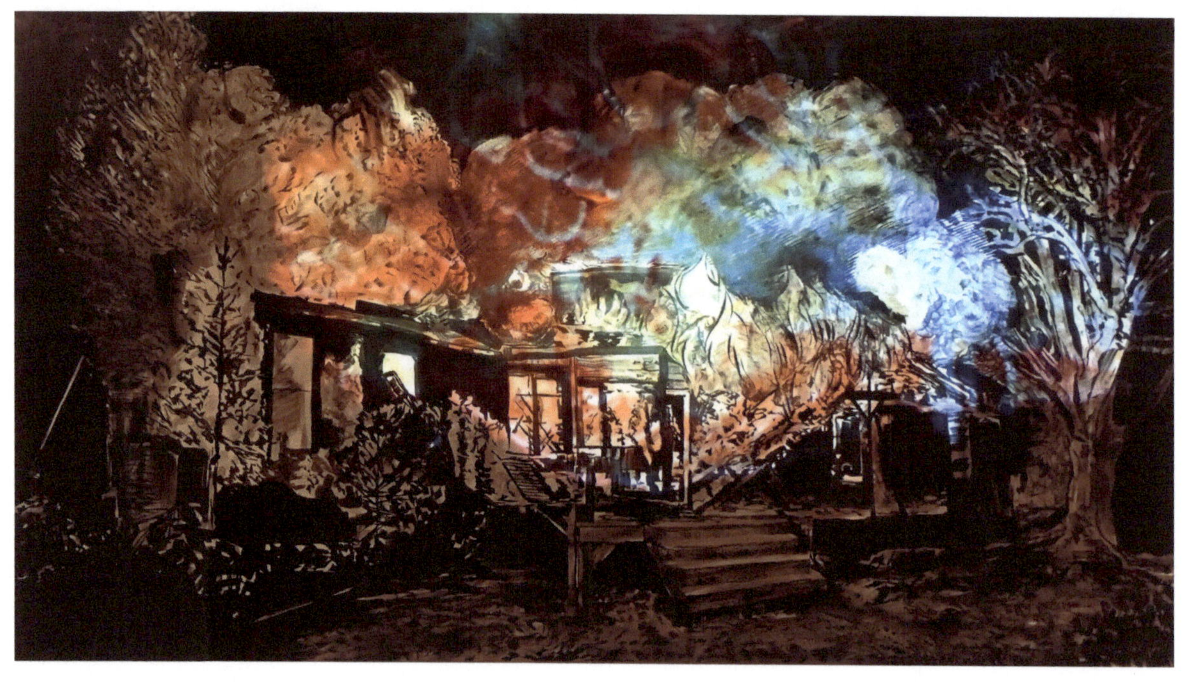

Hollis Hammonds
House on Fire, 2016
Ink on Yupo, Video Projection
60 x 108 in.

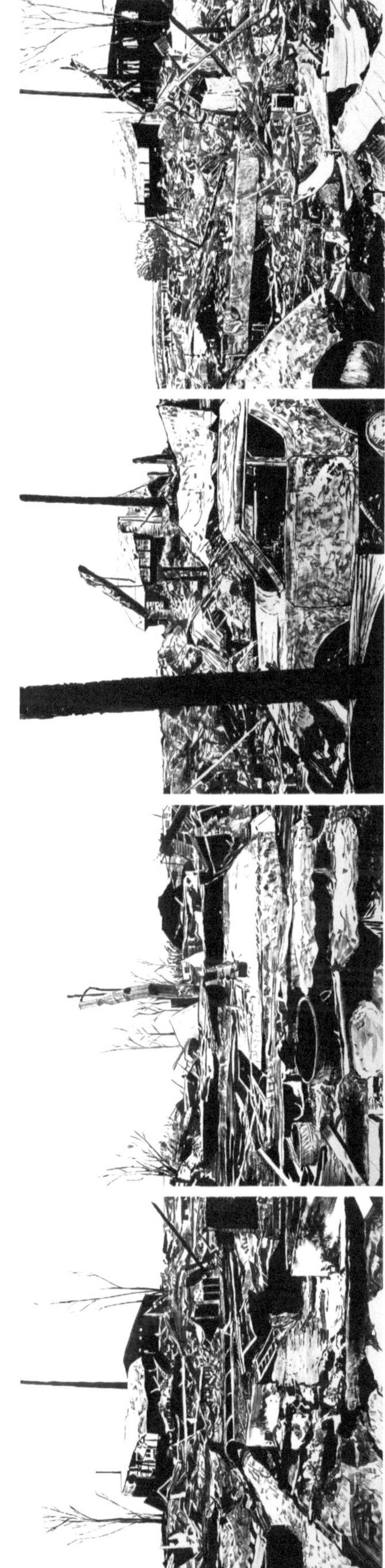

Hollis Hammonds
Wasteland, 2016
Ink on Yupo,
60 x 246 in.

Peter Hiatt

Denton, Texas   peterhiatt.com

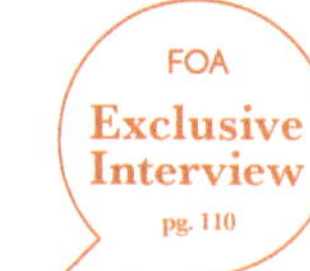

"There are no unsacred places; there are only sacred places and desecrated places."
– Wendell Berry

In the vast stretches of suburbia in which many Americans live, retail centers are a common feature of the landscape. They are built next to houses, office buildings, and restaurants. They are a regular feature in everyday life, because of their proximity and proliferation, and because they are the subject of frequent, required visits for groceries, clothes, and other goods. For many people in contemporary society, their daily lives consist primarily of visits to their home, their workplace, and retail centers. Throughout all of these experiences, their interaction with the land they inhabit is interrupted by a sheet of concrete.

Retail centers are an example of what Marc Augé calls Non-places. In his book Non-Places: An Introduction to Supermodernity, Augé describes Non-places as places that have no connection to history, culture, or identity. They are spaces designed for people to move through, such as an airport, highway, or supermarket. In a retail store, a customer is instructed, through text,

spatial cues, and learned societal behavior, to move through the space, collect goods, and exit the space after paying. This direction of movement is a core part of the power structure that allows a retail center to exist. CONTINUED ON PAGE 95 →

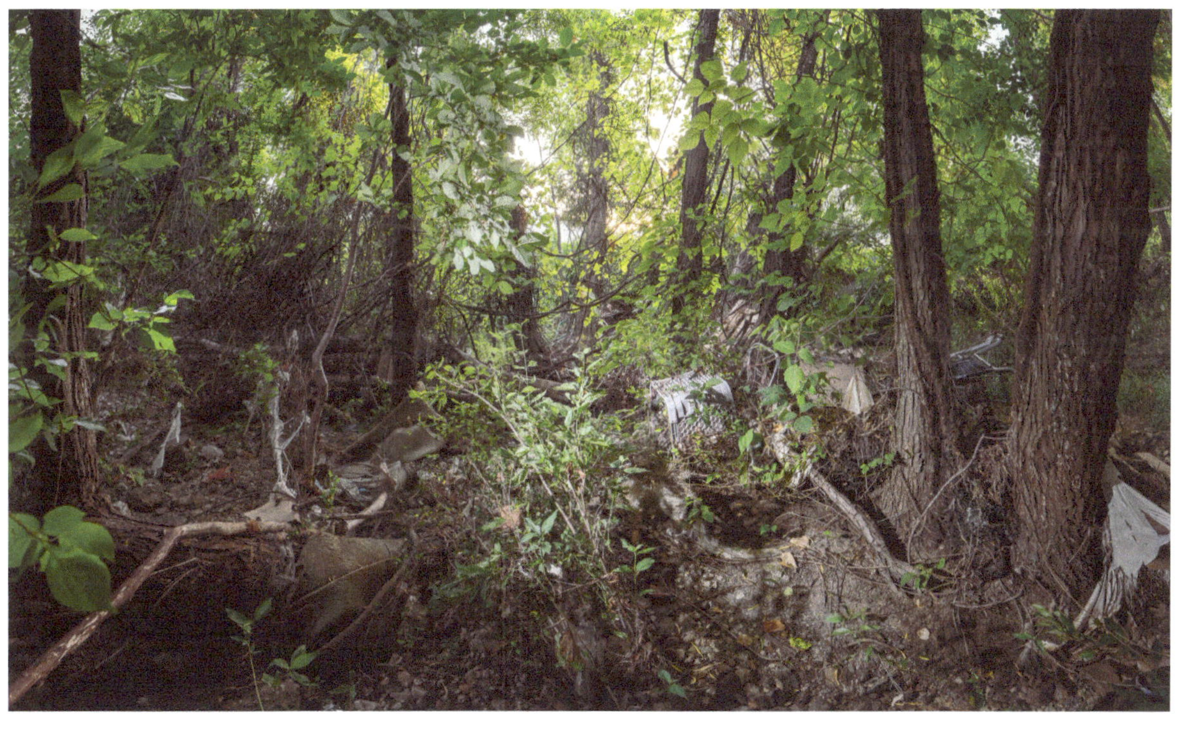

Peter Hiatt
Behind Pier 1 Imports, 2016
Archival Pigment Print,
18 x 32 in.

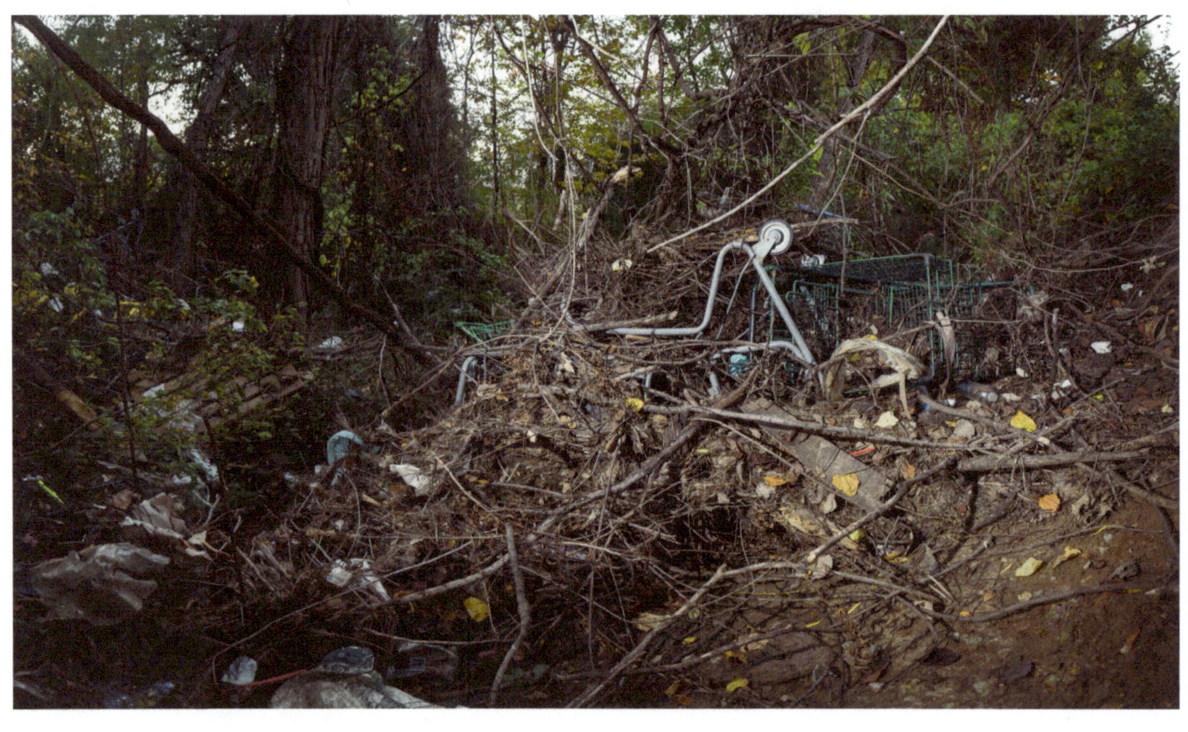

Peter Hiatt
Behind Michaels, 2016
Archival Pigment Print.
18 x 32 in.

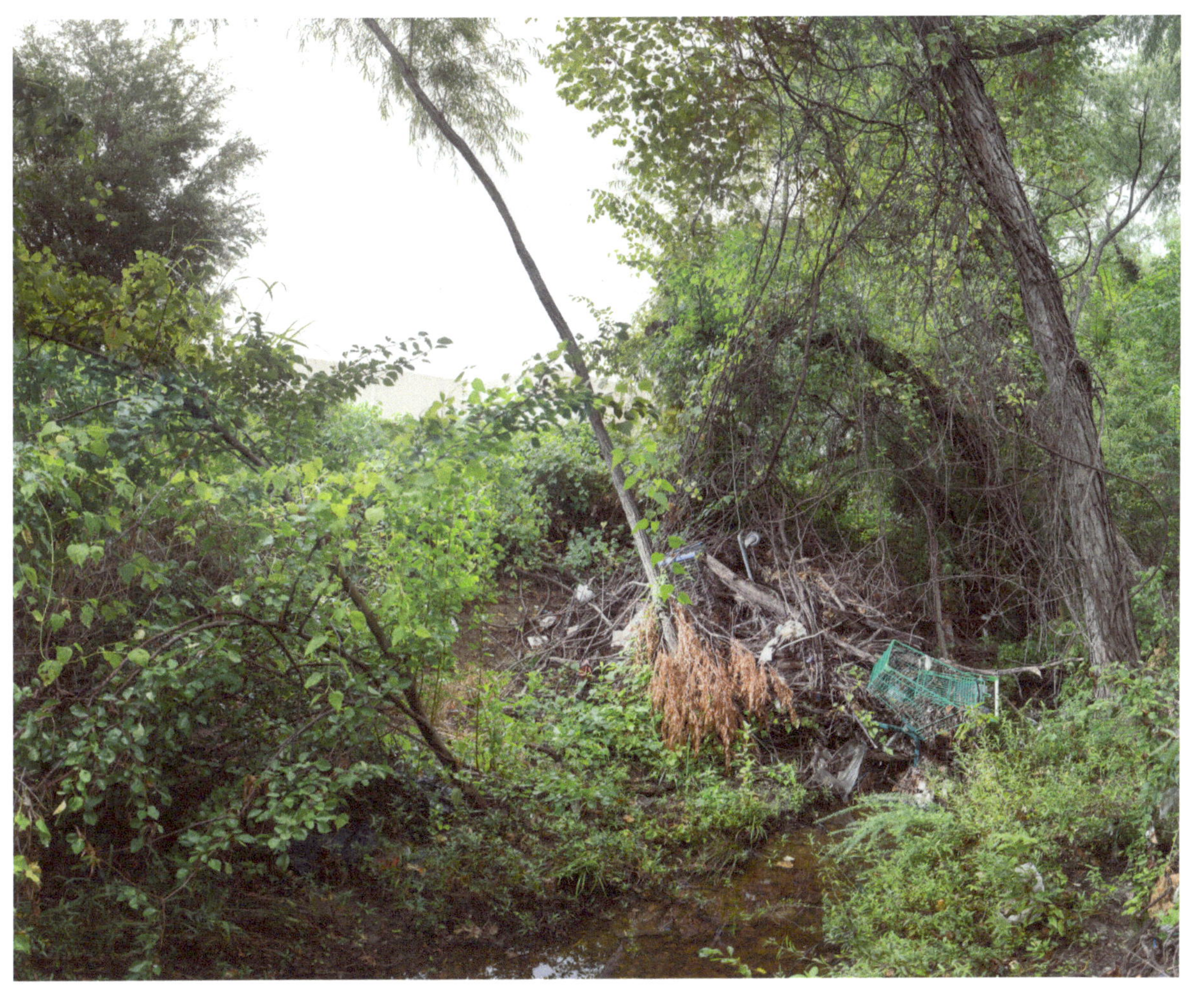

Peter Hiatt
Behind Pier 1 Imports IV, 2016
Archival Pigment Print,
18 x 22.5 in.

Hannah Hill   *Brooklyn, New York*   hannahhillart.com

On a back-road, her bike sat untouched, sinking into a muddy ditch. Her door was ajar. Fingerprint dust covered countertops and light switches. The lights in her house came on less and less. I have memories of these things but never witnessed them—a paradigm referred to in psychology as "crashing memories." I was told where they found her bike and that I was one of the last to see her, when in all probability, I imagined it. Gardai walked between our home and hers. Hushed voices and radio chatter. When her body was found, speculations morphed into recollections. I imagined grasping hands and clawing nails, the awkward maneuvering of her body into his trunk and the glow of headlights as she was tossed over the rocky cliffs.

When I tell them about the origin of Sunrise on Fanore Beach (my painting that reads to some as a mountain range, to others a body bag), my former housemates don't immediately recall our neighbor's murder. It was tragic, but to us passing, peripheral. While the details have eroded beyond reliability, there are news articles to remind me that my neighbor Deidre was murdered in 2011. In the way of relics, we are not always so fortunate. Often times an experience, or non-experience, lives on only in faulty memories, bent out of shape, consumed, believed. My work touches on the nature of

reality, of memoir suffused in fantasy and dread. I recall lying on the carpet as a child and telling my dad about my imaginary worlds. He told me that on some plane my worlds were real, simply because I thought them. He explained to me, in dumbed down theory, the question of Schrödinger's Cat.

Years later, my approach is still influenced by this, although the answer to me is that the cat (and memoir) are both alive and dead, true and false, mine and yours—simultaneously. My work follows my memory, crushing it, eroding it—creating a personal mythology.

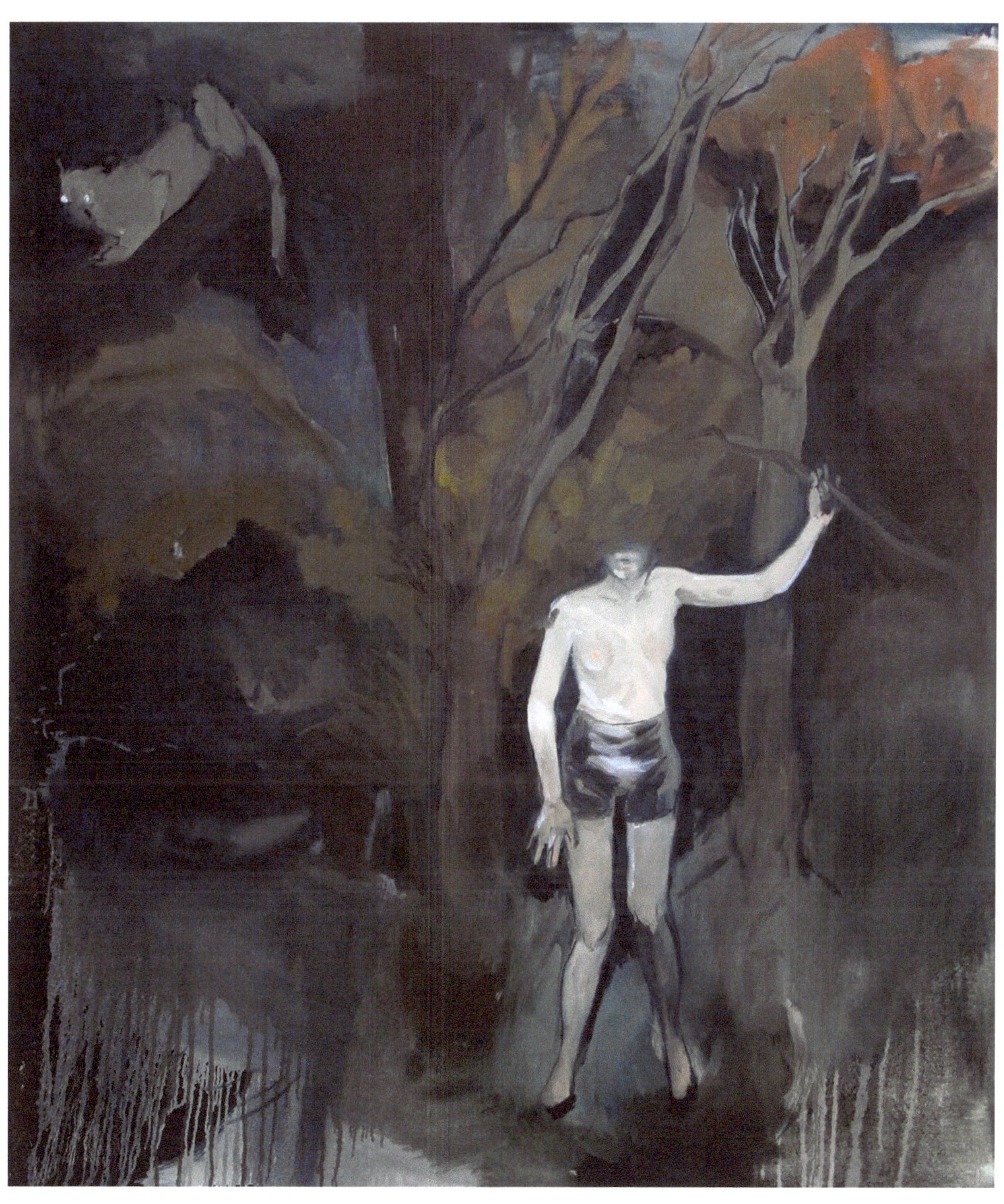

Hannah Hill
Baby Boy She's a Loner, 2016
Oil on canvas,
5 x 5 ft.

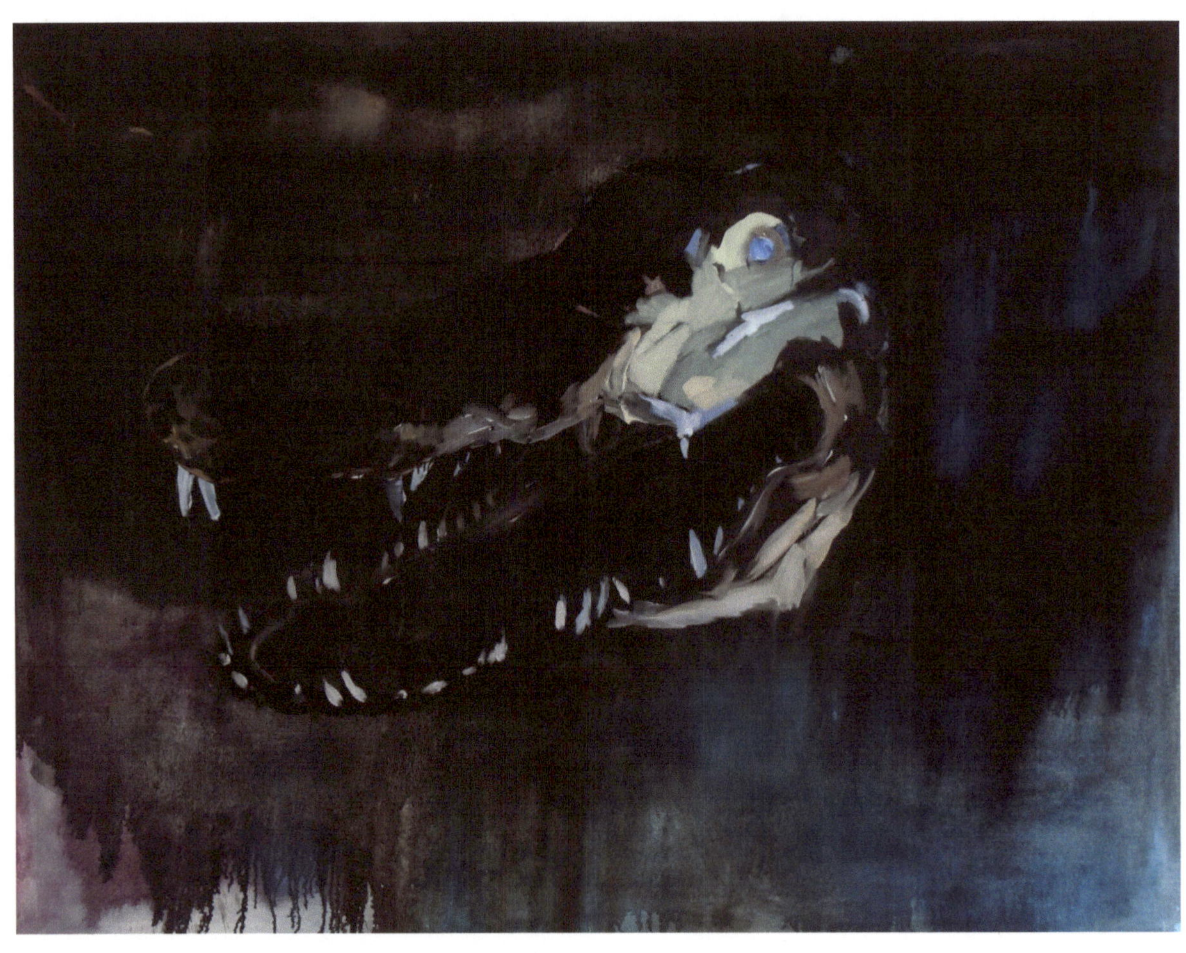

Hannah Hill
Hey bb, 2016
Oil on canvas,
6 x 4 ft.

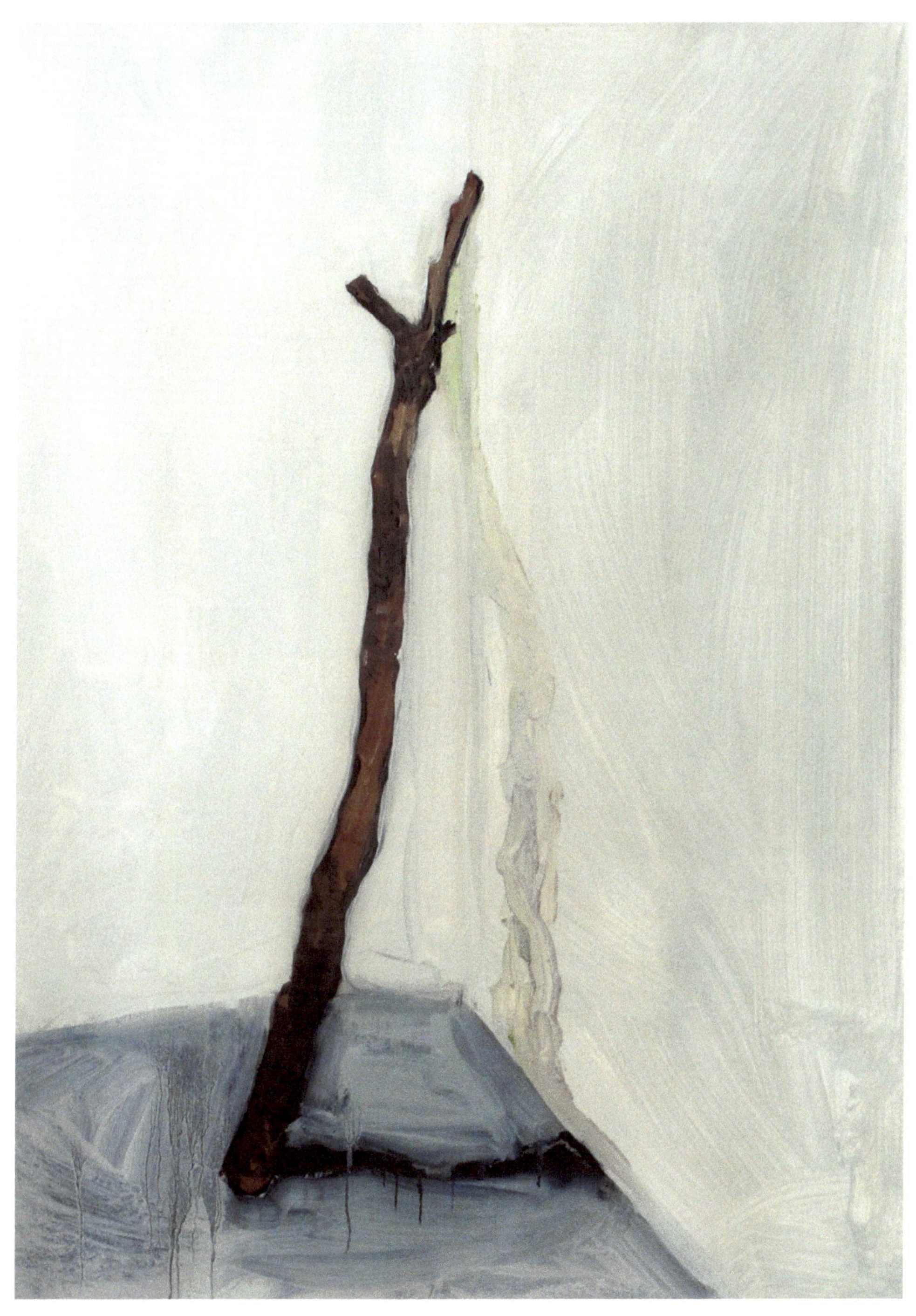

Hannah Hill
Stick, 2016
Oil on paper,
3.5 x 2 ft.

Bambi Johnson *Melbourne, Australia* bambi-johnson.com

Bambi is a Melbourne based mixed media artist working across the mediums of sculpture, illustration, and print media. Her varied work is thematically driven by a desire to express natural compulsions of contemporary feminism. Within her sculptural mixed media works, Bambi draws on the unconscious body to indemnify experience through transference. Her use of photographic media promotes the purity of constructed, soft, sculptured objects whilst enabling a shift in dimensions, creating a singular and consumable perspective.

Often her soft sculptures operate with an alluring subtlety. Sexually suggestive and constructed with passive materials such as sand, panty hose, wax and twine, the scale is set to immerse and evoke sentimental inquiry between appeal & disdain.

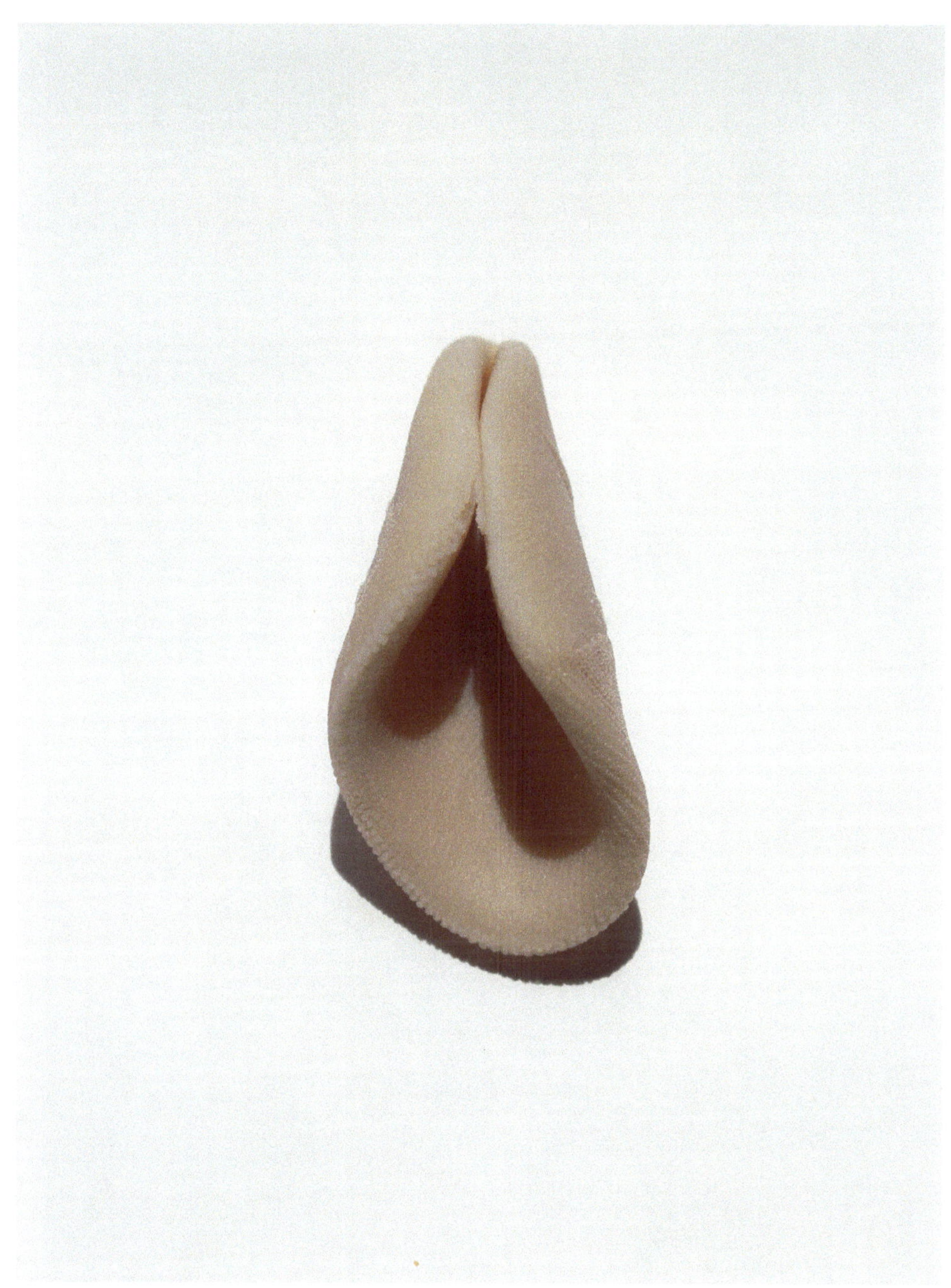

Bambi Johnson
Cookie, 2017
Inkjet on rag,
594 x 841 cm.

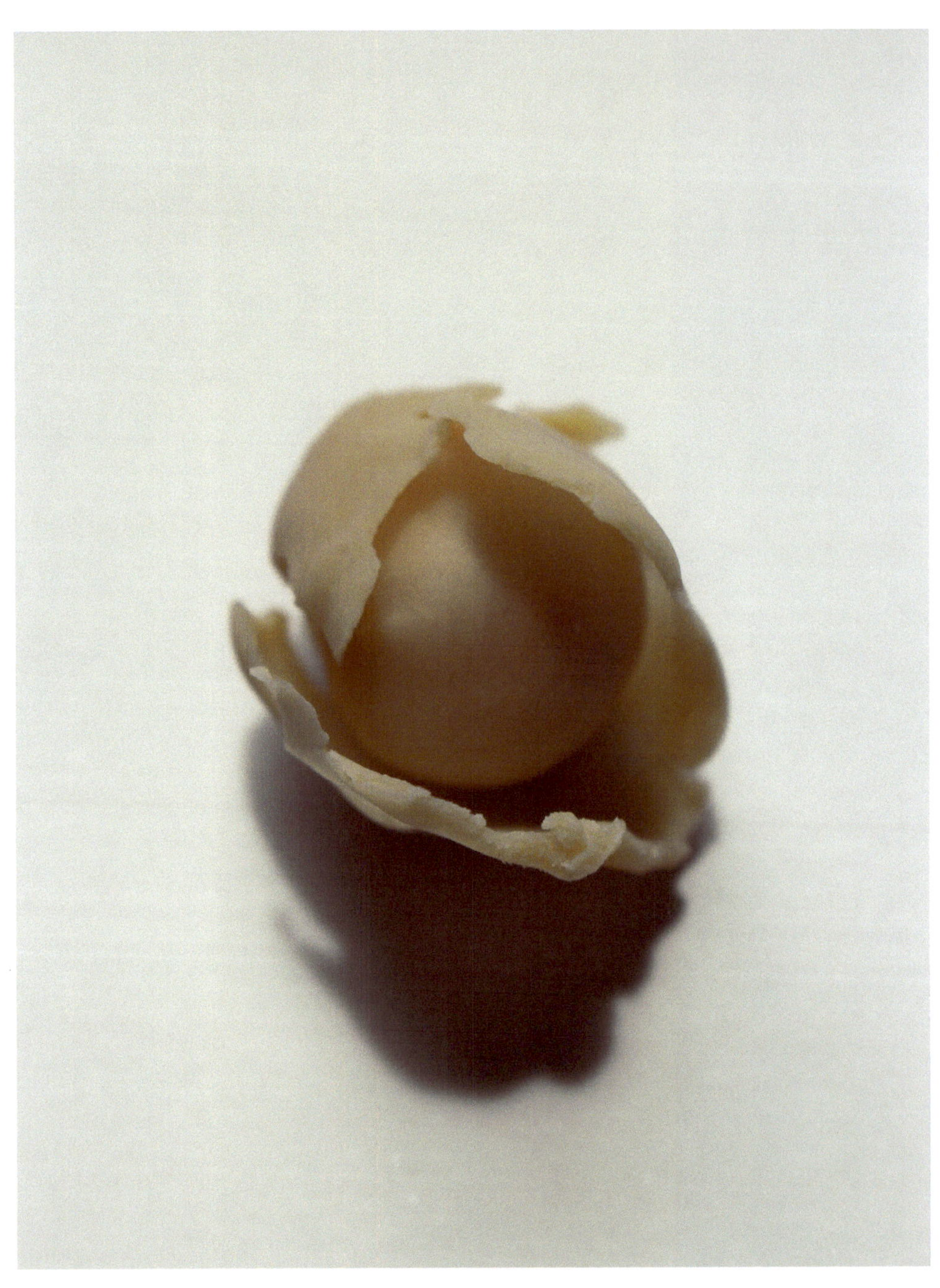

Bambi Johnson
Embryology, 2017
Inkjet on rag,
594 x 841 cm.

Friend of The Artist

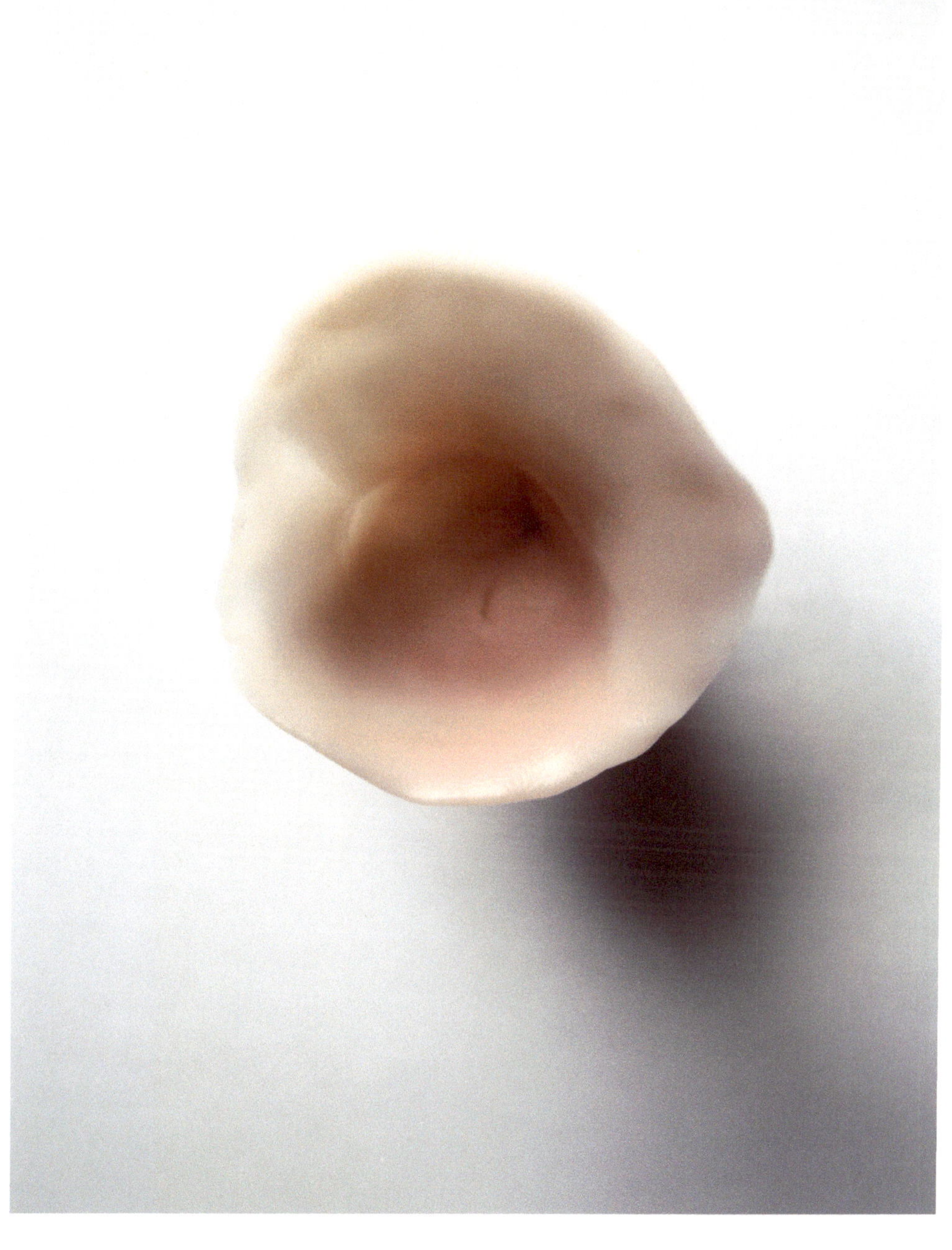

Bambi Johnson
Embryology, 2017
Inkjet on rag,
594 x 841 cm.

Bonam Kim

Brooklyn, New York   bonamkim.com

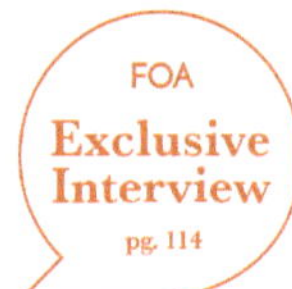

Since moving from Seoul, experiences of displacement and my struggle with cultural identity cause me to see things differently. In this unfamiliar space, my sense of self is both threatened and emancipated. I cannot escape the need for psychological dependency, nostalgic desires, and memories that seem to guarantee security and comfort.

My work starts here.

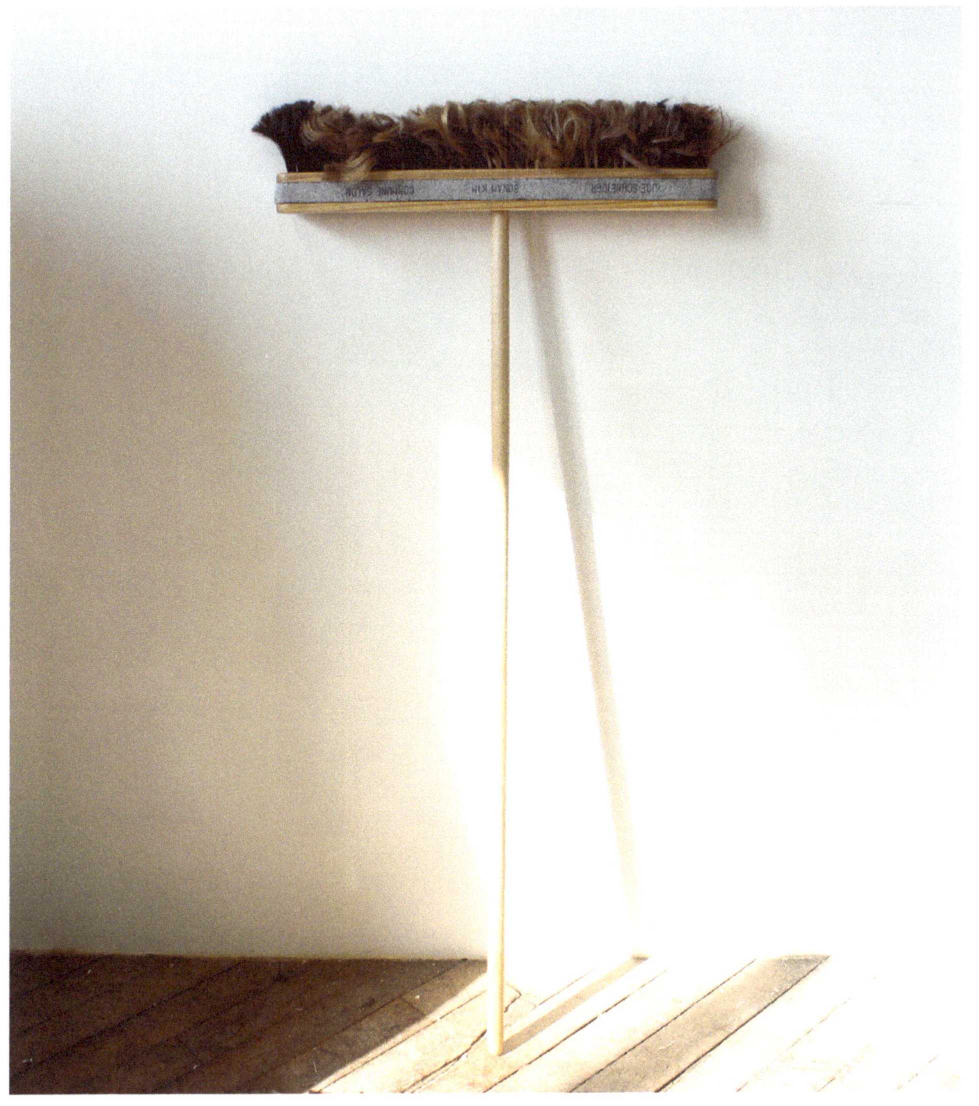

Bonam Kim
Broom Project (series #1), 2016
Wood, resin, human hair,
12 x 12 in.

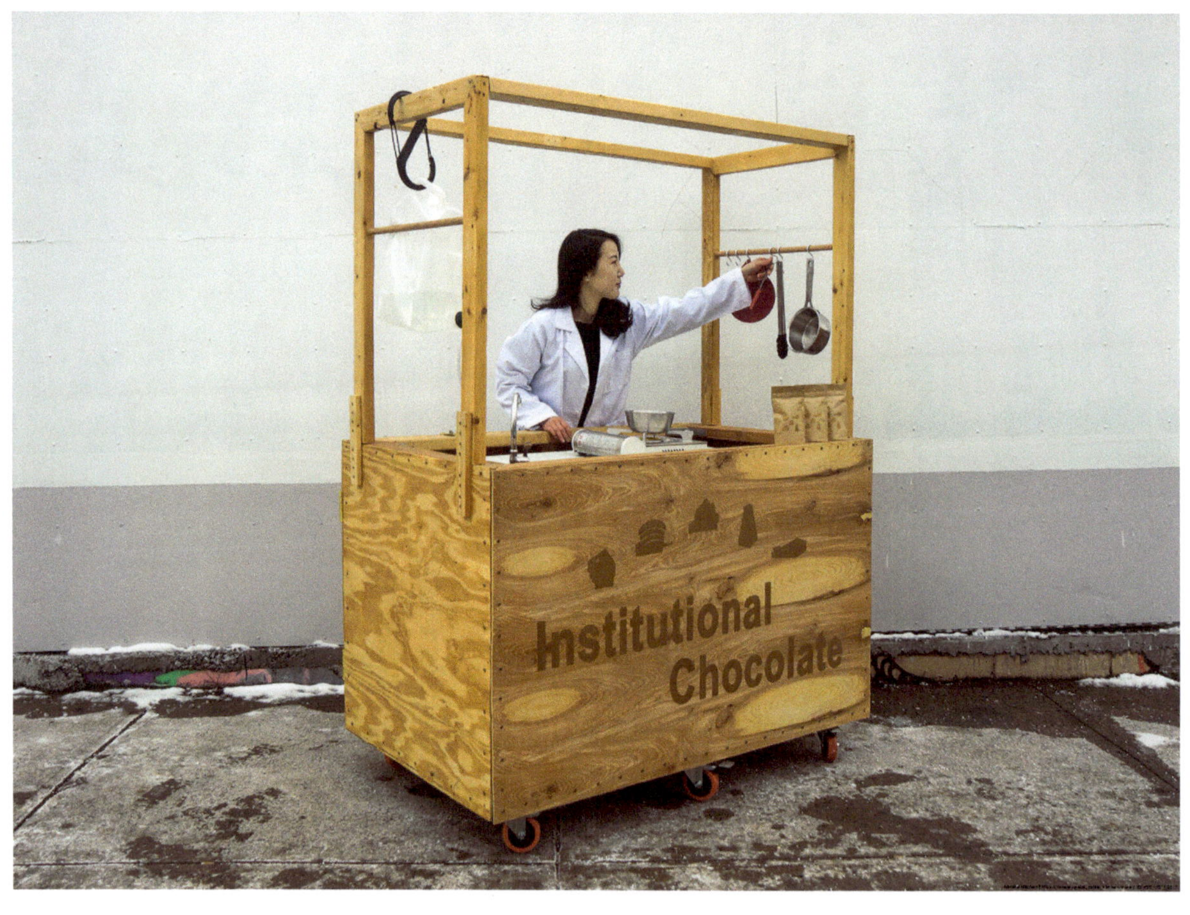

Bonam Kim
Mobile Kitchen, 2017
Wood, wheel, paint, table,
kitchen ware,
33 x 55 x 75 in.

Friend of The Artist

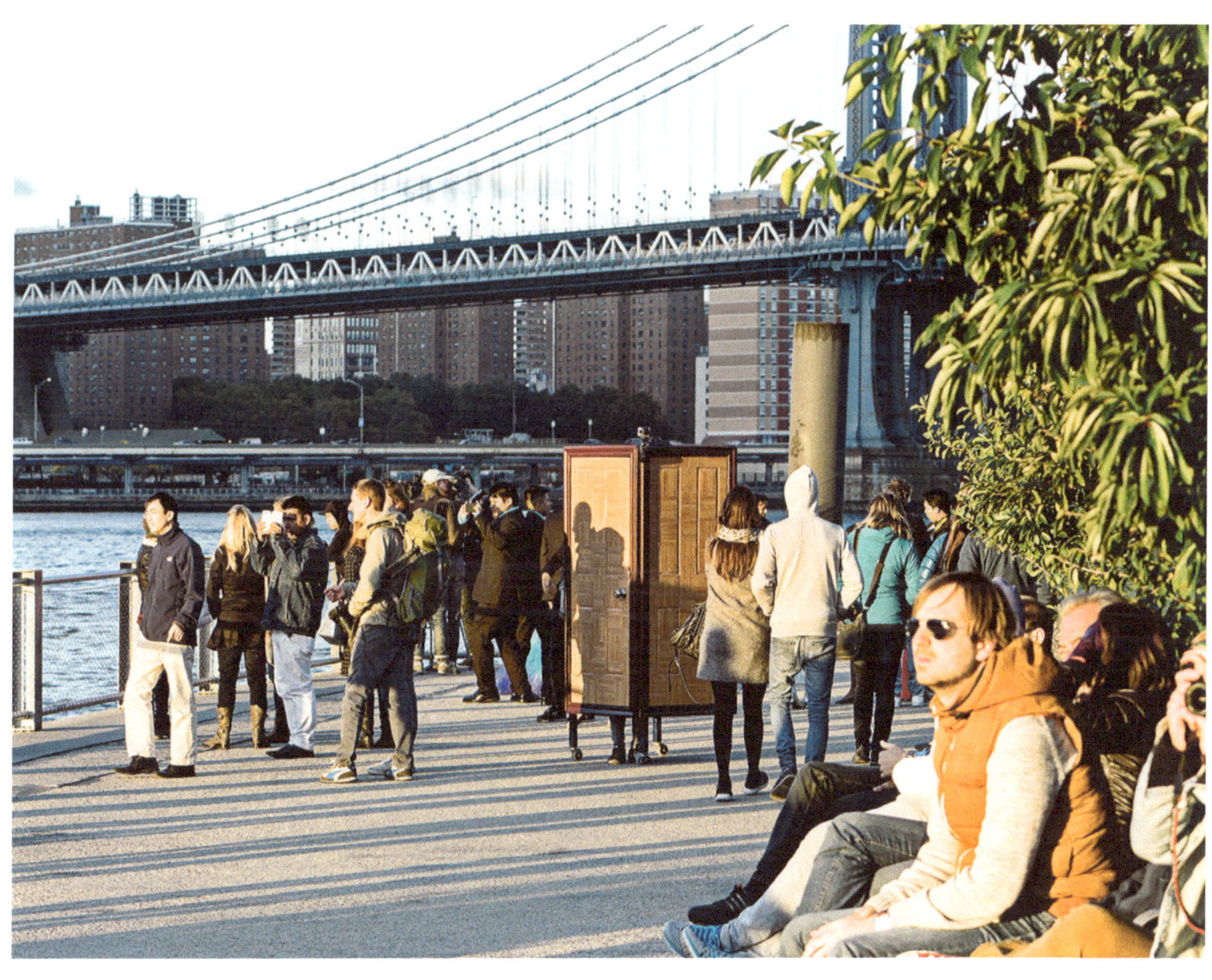

Bonam Kim
Through the crack, 2015
Wood, hinge, wheel, floor sheet, insulated foam,
35 x 35 x 77 in.
4 minutes 58 seconds video

Justin Korver   *San Antonio, Texas*   justinkorver.com

With the art in The Expressive Mark & Other Ideas I Stole from Painting I wanted to continue my work with tools. I'm interested in tools because they are extensions of us, and like the things we surround ourselves with they act as still life. These tools are meant to express an absent subject, much like the Dutch still life where breakfast has been laid out but the eater is curiously absent. We may, therefore, invent our own subject or possibly become the subject of these types of still life. My suspicion is that within my work, when we imagine the hand that fills the work glove, swings the hammer, or grips the pliers we often imagine a male hand. Of course, we should not exclusively imagine men as the only possible users of tools because women are as capable of using a tool skillfully. But I am compelled by our default to tools as masculine things. Another proof we might look to is the pejorative use of tool. If I was to call someone a tool, my subject would generally be male. He is acting without thought or regard. We might think this individual is completely filled with action to the exclusion of thought or empathy; we might also be saying that he is a phallus or a dick. "Tool" is often used to allude to the male genital. In all these cases, maleness is described in terms of what it does. Maleness, like "toolness,"

is a case where form follows function. The term "form follows function" is perhaps the great mantra of modern architecture & design and was coined by the functionalist architect, Louis Sullivan. So a hammer's form is a transcription of its use. The handle is long so it can provide leverage, the head concentrates the force down to a relatively small area, and the claws at the back allow for nails to be forcefully wrenched free. In all cases, the hammer is an action in search of a subject. The hammer is looking for a nail.

CONTINUED ON PAGE 95 →

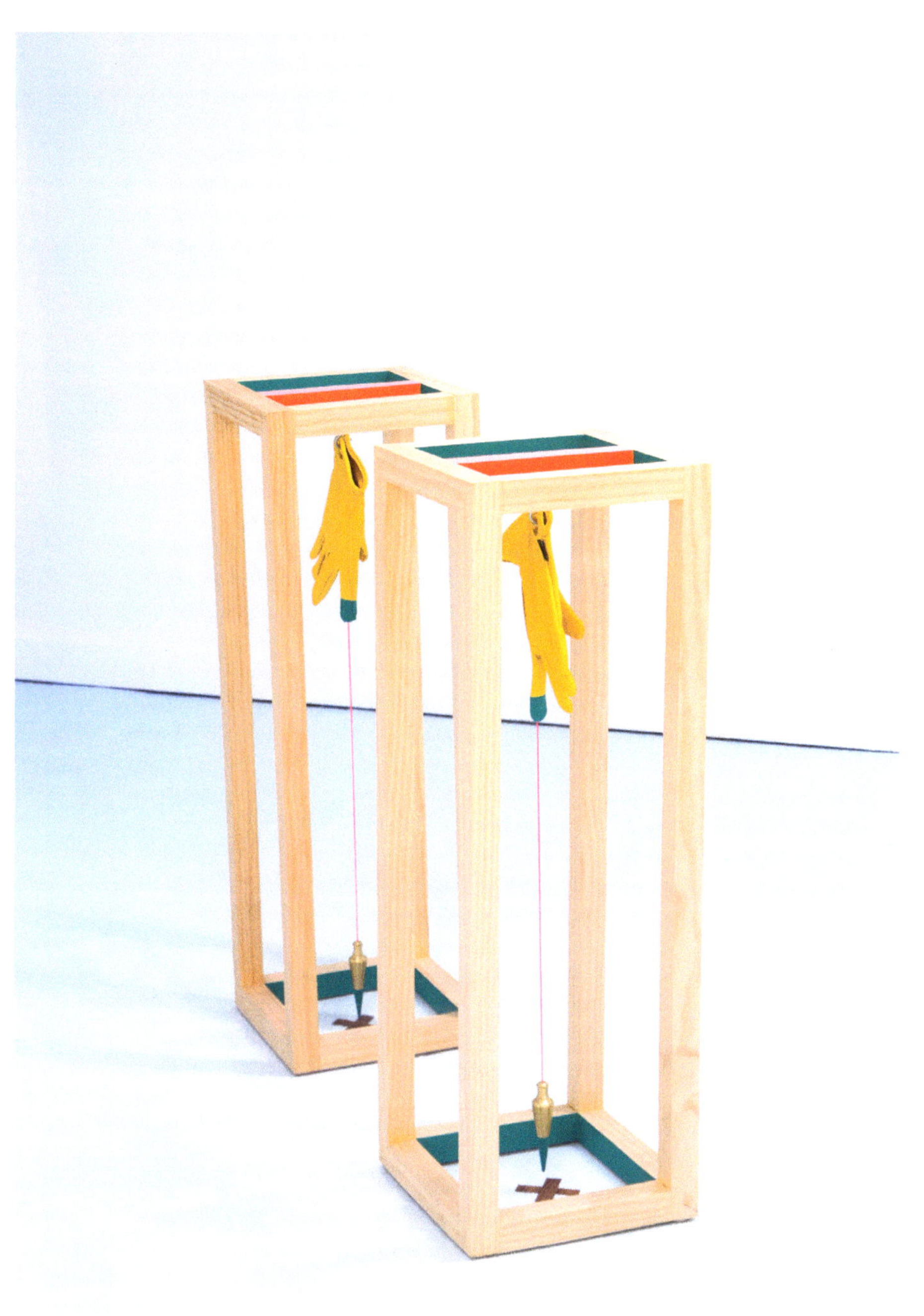

Justin Korver
Plumb or Straight Line, 2017
Pine, paint, string, gloves, plumb bob,
vinyl,
36 1/4 x 12 x 38 in.

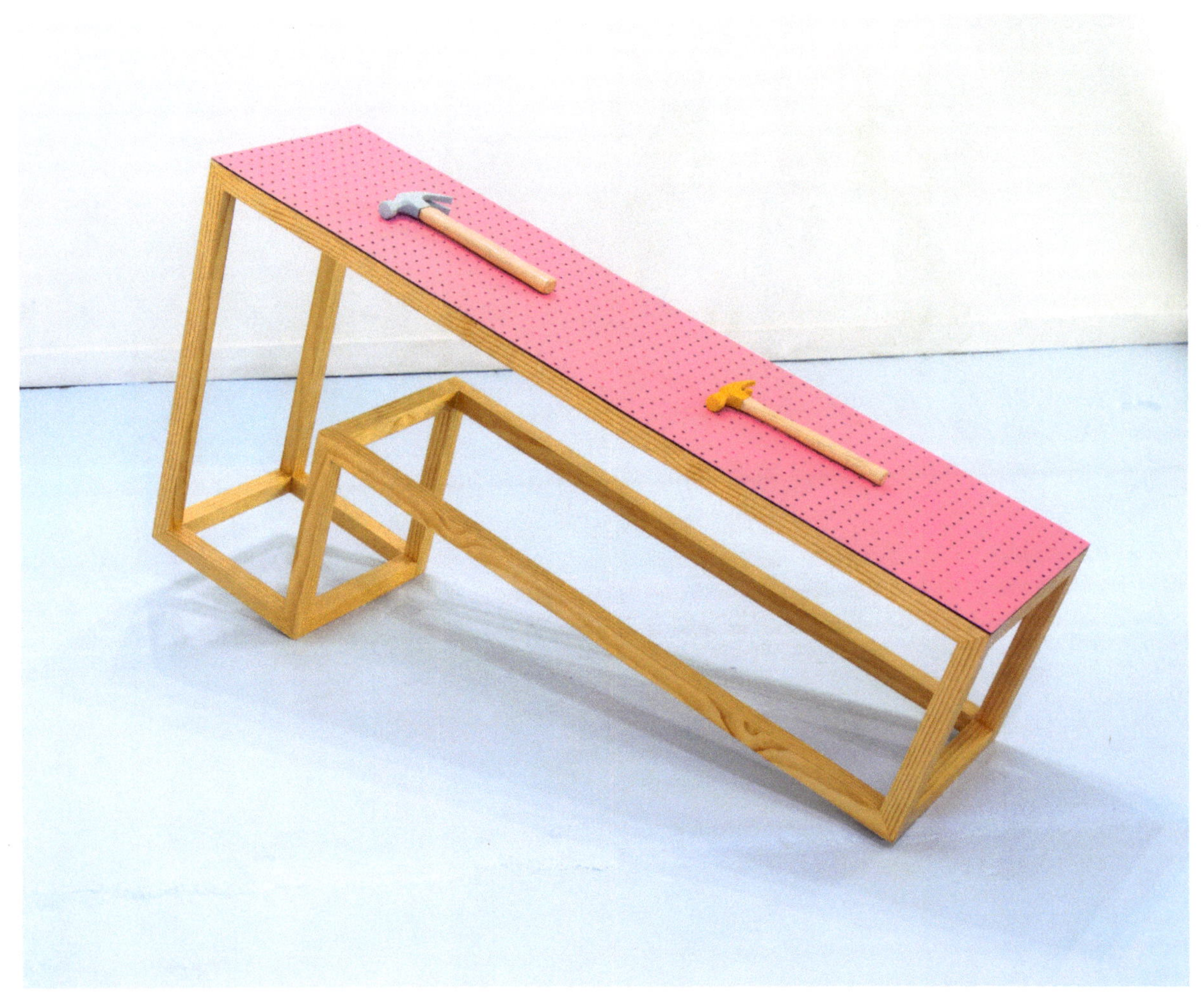

Justin Korver
Big Tool, Little Tool, 2016
Pegboard, Pine, paint, hammers,
66 x 15 x 33 1/2 in.

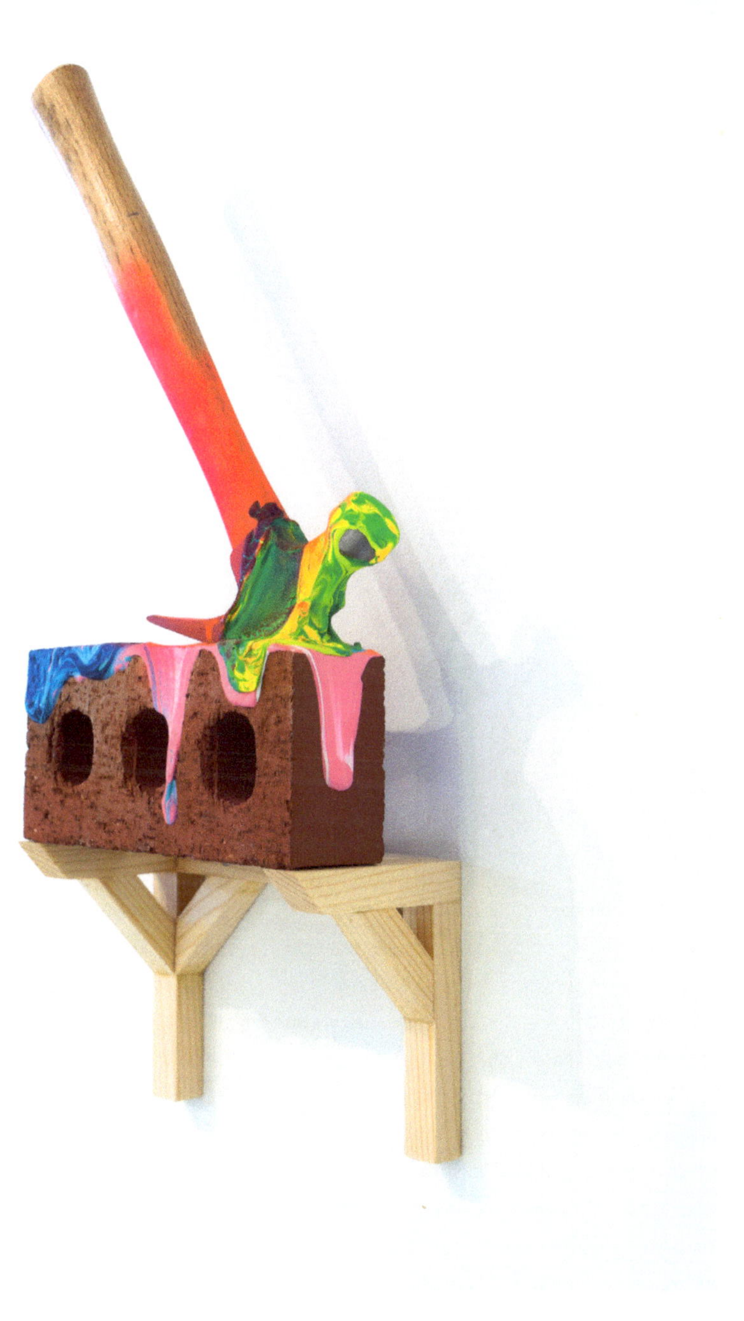

Justin Korver
Relating or the Cliche of a Rock and a
Hard Place, 2017
Pine, screws, brick, paint, hammer,
21 x 9 x 4 1/4 in.

Maria Kostareva *Moscow, Russia*   m-kostareva.com

I see my work as a tool for instilling mindfulness into everyday life. I focus on all those mundane spaces, actions and images that make up our daily existence. Even casual passers-by of Moscow's many underpasses secure a place in my memory as bearers of meaning. My art works reveal what we see when we don't look. My own reality is constructed of a good many daily routines like washing up or combing my hair. Being repeated hundreds and thousands of times every-day, these actions start to be seen as devoid of essence. In an attempt to cope with the hectic pace of a big city, I strive for mindfulness through capturing and bringing to life those images that normally endure only for a short while. The composition of my artworks is based on the principle of an accidental photo. The figures appear on the canvas, just as they would to a human eye, only partly. There are no faces in my pictures, except for my own, reflected in a mirror, which leaves the passers-by unrecognized and silent. The images do not unfold into a narrative: they are nothing but the moments appropriated from eternity.

I use contrasting elements to convey the pulsation of this endless dance the figures and the space are engaged in: forming a single whole one moment, taking distance from each other the next. I do not draw from nature and the entire work has been done from memory. This way I ensure that the forms, having been appropriated and in a way transformed by my memory, have become my own.

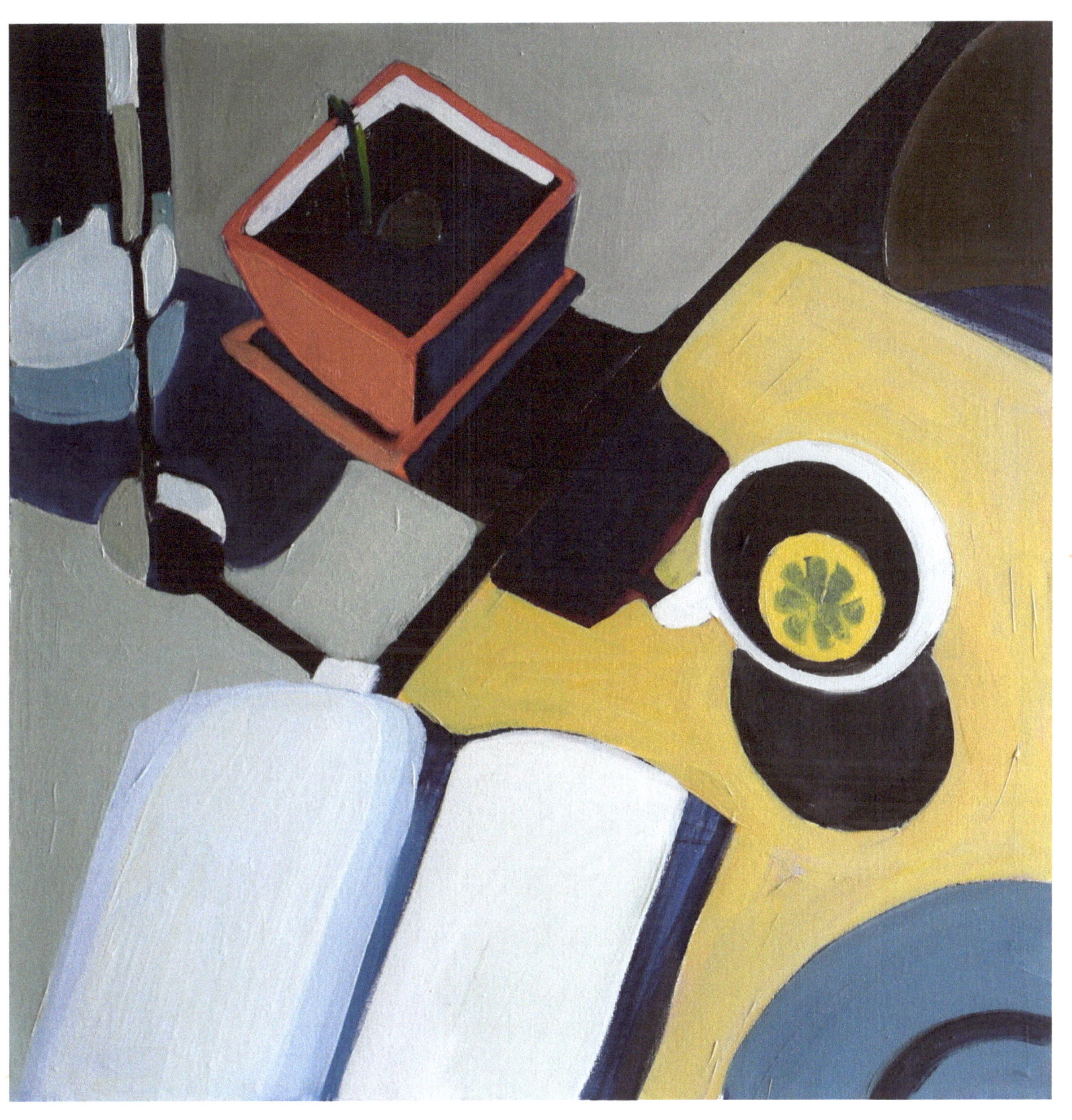

Maria Kostareva
10:01 a.m., 2017
Oil on canvas,
50 x 50 cm.

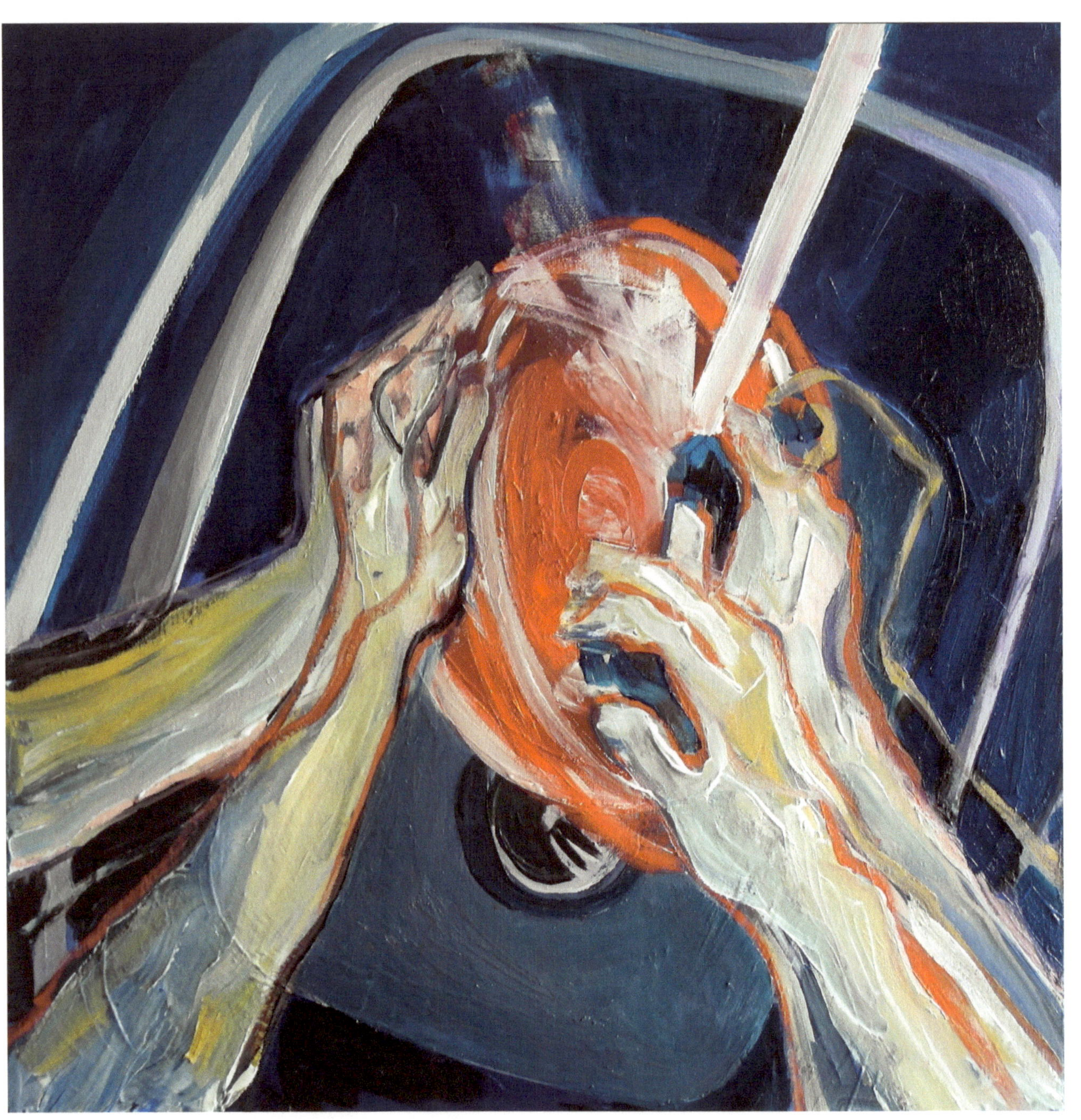

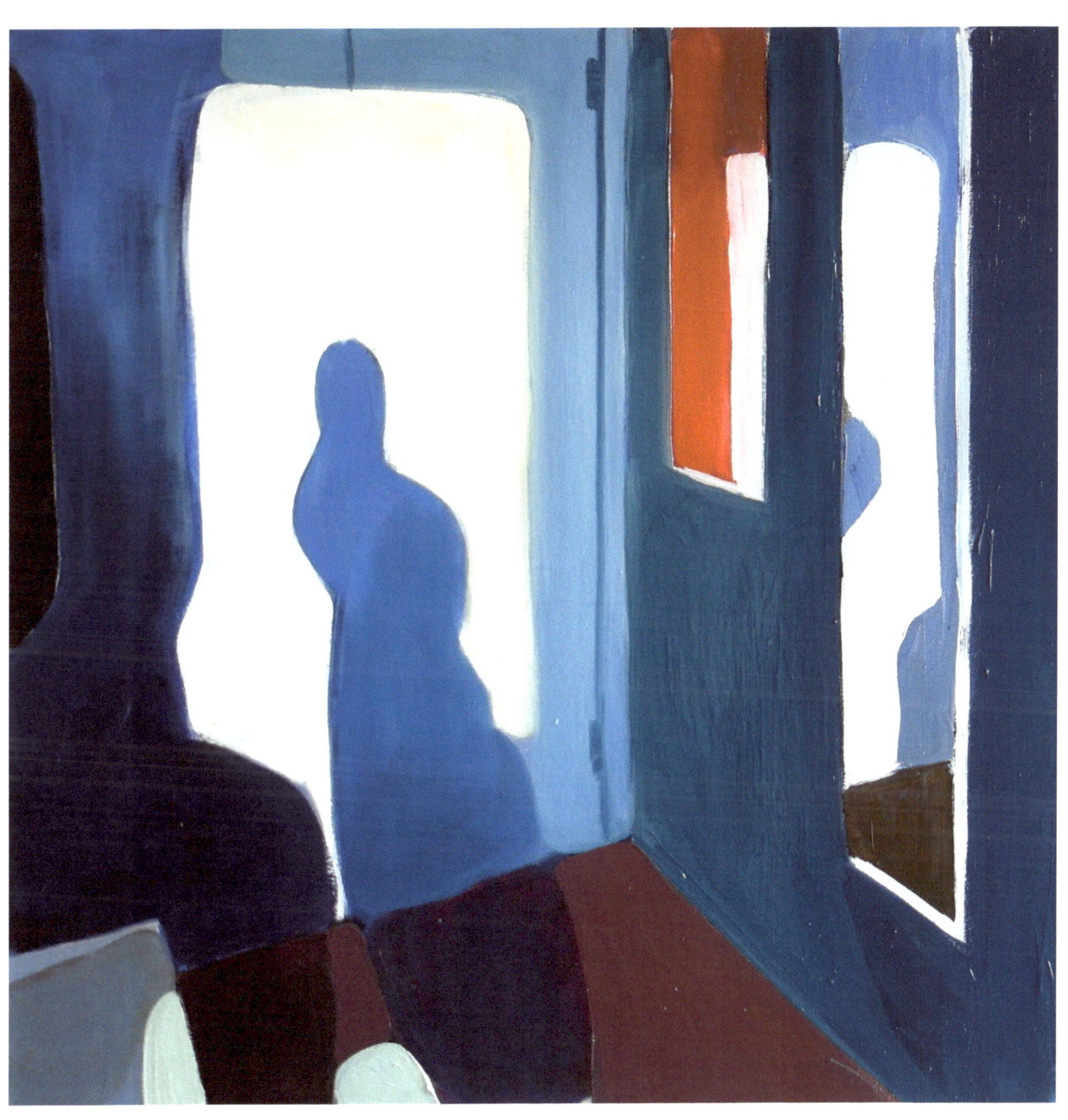

Maria Kostareva
Before Sunset, 2017
Oil on canvas,
50 x 50 cm.

Ryan Montgomery

Austin, Texas

sandisonmontgomery.com

Ryan Sandison Montgomery is an artist currently living and working in Austin, TX whose paintings live in the intersection of sentimentality and anxiety. Montgomery is a graduate of Pratt Institute, with a BFA in experimental film, and worked for a decade in high-end window display on 5th and Madison Avenues. He is a relatively recent transplant to Austin, having moved to Texas from New York in 2014.

Nutrition Facts is an ongoing series of large oil paintings exploring foods that are personally meaningful, and also have regional or cultural significance. Taste is used as a vehicle for memory, as well as local and dead brands, family recipes and secret ingredients. In the same way that languages die off as the world becomes more connected, and accents fade as the country becomes smaller, food and our evolving relationship to it can symbolize the bittersweet nature of cultural and global change.

Montgomery's abstract pieces are pure heart-to-hand works or "glorified doodles," something like the automatic writing of a skeptic.

The artist's painting Buttermilk Pie was recently awarded the "People's Choice Award 2016" by the City of Austin. It was purchased by the city for its permanent collection and resides in City Hall.

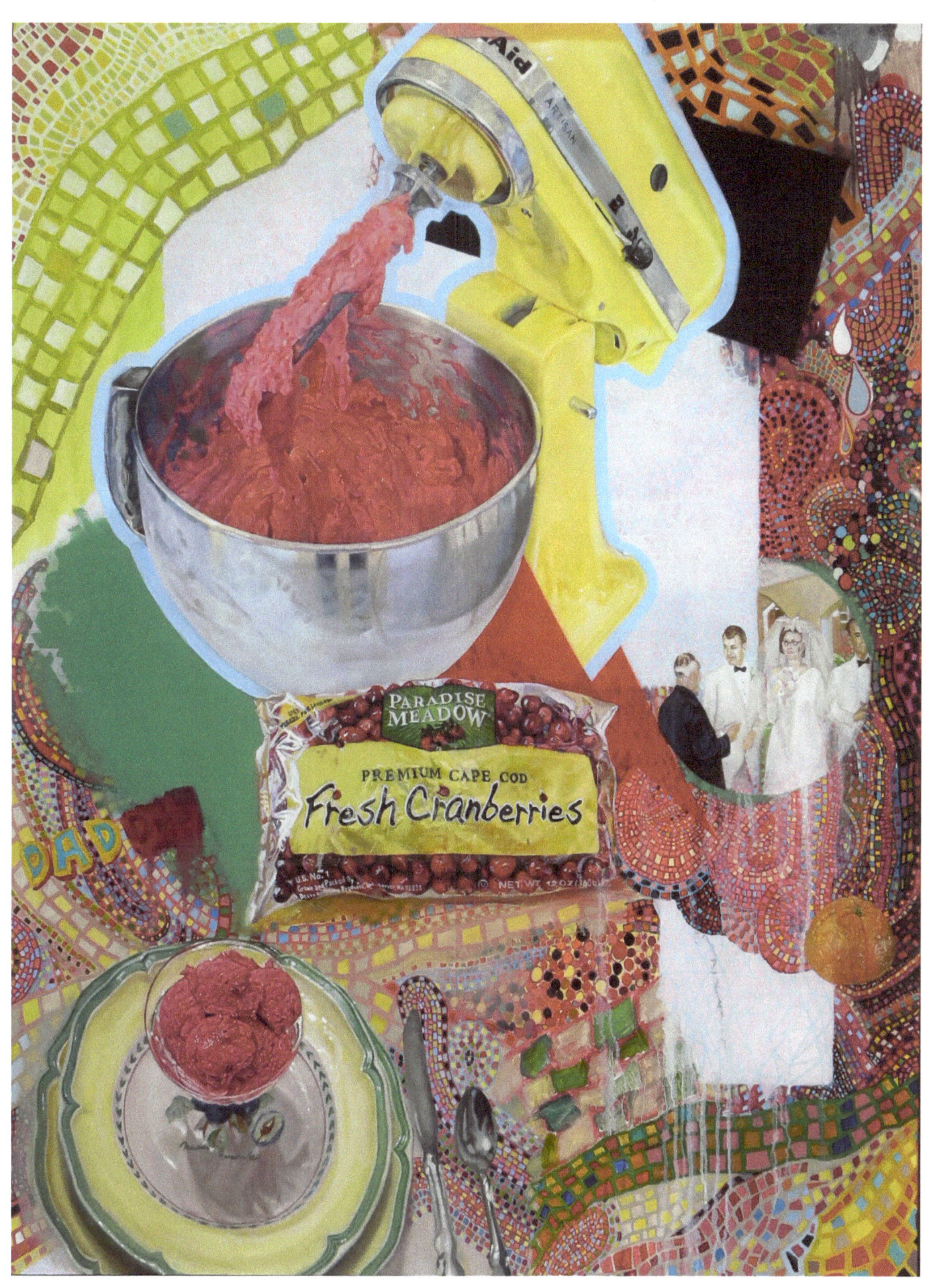

Ryan Montgomery
Cranberry Ice, 2016
Oil on canvas,
36 x 48 in.

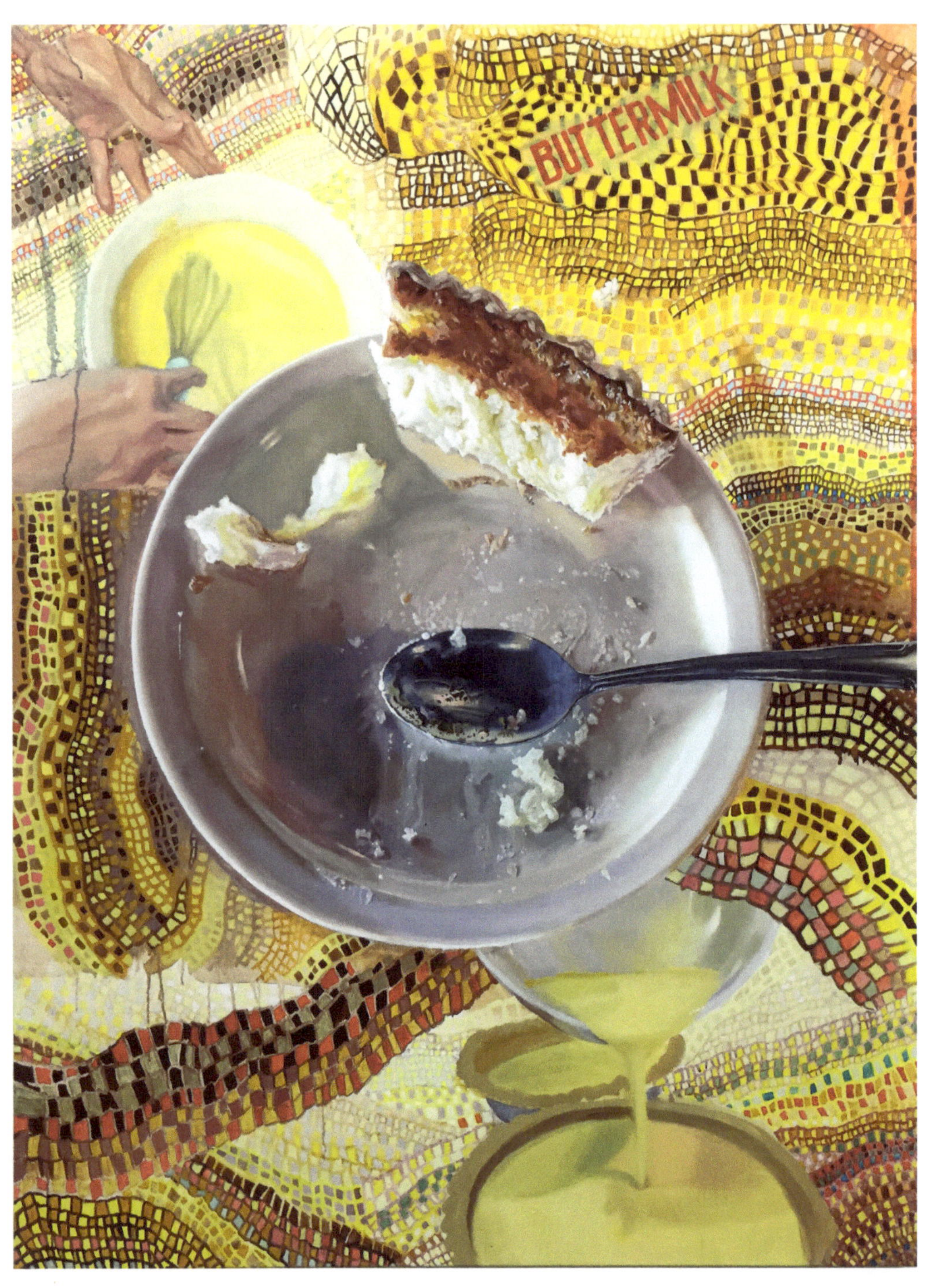

Ryan Montgomery
Buttermilk Pie, 2015
Oil on canvas,
36 x 48 in.

Friend of The Artist

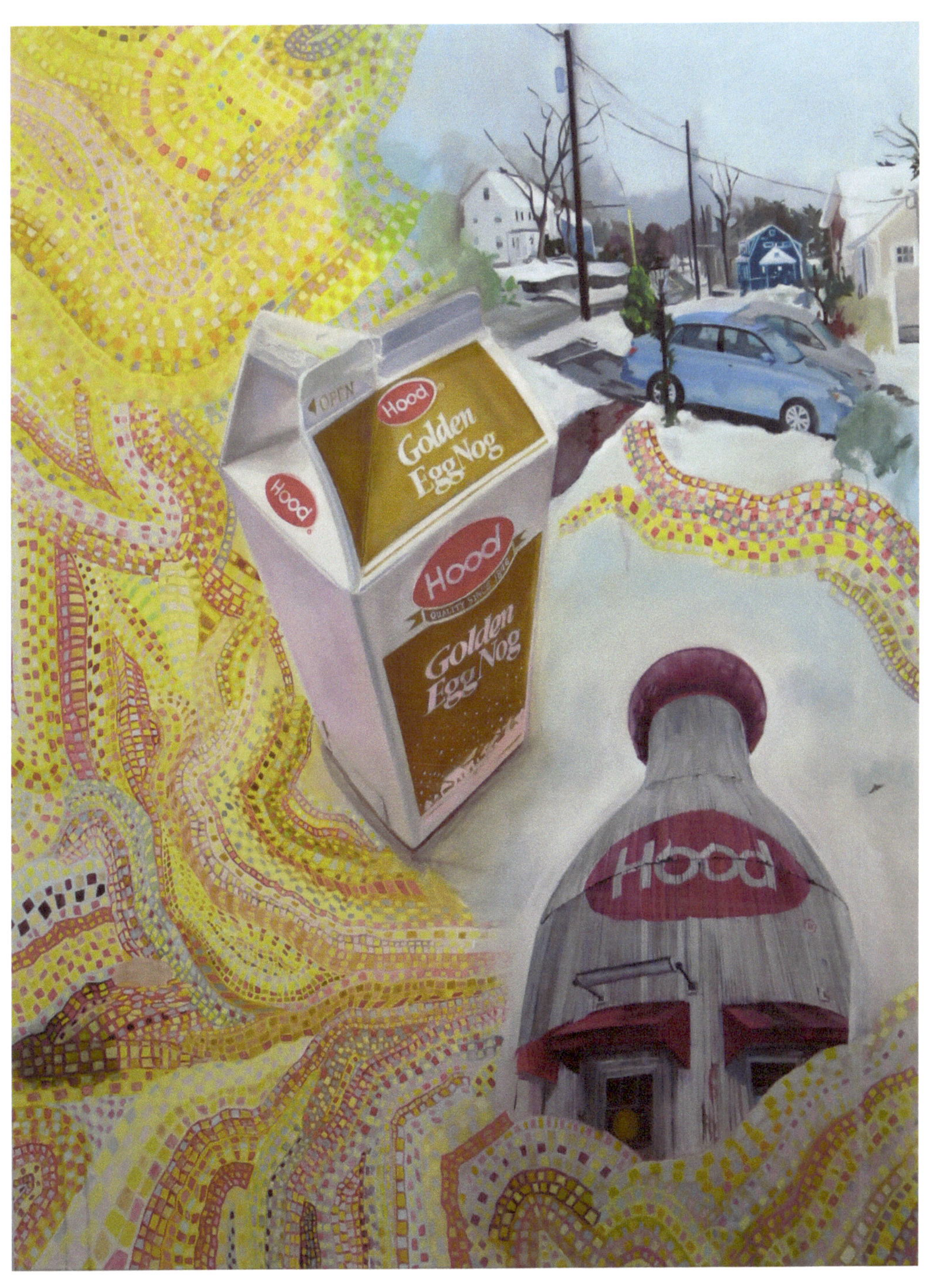

Ryan Montgomery
Egg Nog, 2016
Oil on canvas,
36 x 48 in.

Isabelle O'Donnell *Portland, Maine*

isabelleodonnell.com

My work is concerned with pattern, color, and texture, as well as the continuing conversations concerning materiality and textiles as a means to explore and question painting abstraction. I draw influence from my personal history, traditional craft processes, the natural world, and the saturated palette of mass-produced consumer products. My practice as an artist is indebted to a wide range of historical and contemporary artists who questioned and explored ideas of material, abstraction, process, and feminism. I look to the fiber and post-minimalist artists of the 1960s and 70s, as well as the feminist and pattern & decoration arts movements, and the array of contemporary artists whose work deals with process, hand crafts, and painting abstraction. As a female artist, particularly one who uses fiber, it is important to understand my historical precedence within these movements as a struggle to legitimize not only the materials and processes of textiles, but the work of female artists. The struggles of these artists were not only linked to these materials and processes, but their association with femininity, the domestic, and the decorative—all seen through the modernist lens as antithesis to high art.

My work continues and expands upon these explorations through the combination and contrast of the varying mediums and processes of textiles and painting. This is visible through my use of both traditional painting surfaces and techniques in combination with textiles processes such as weaving, dyeing, and sewing.

CONTINUED ON PAGE 96 →

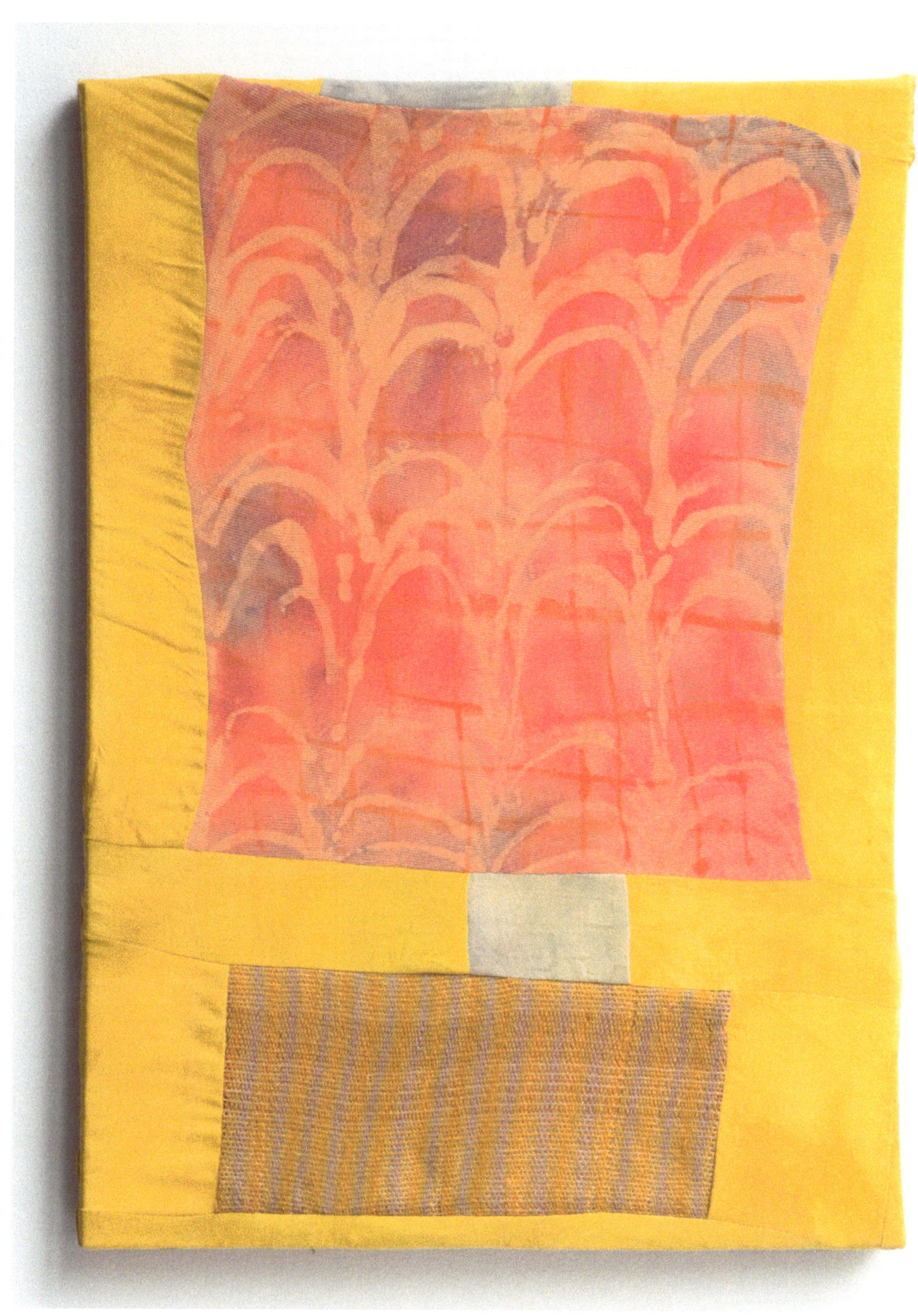

Isabelle O'Donnell
Seedling Conveyor, 2017
Turmeric, Matcha green tea, black tea,
fabric paint, resist, cotton fabric, hand
woven wool, 18 1/2 x 25 1/2 in.

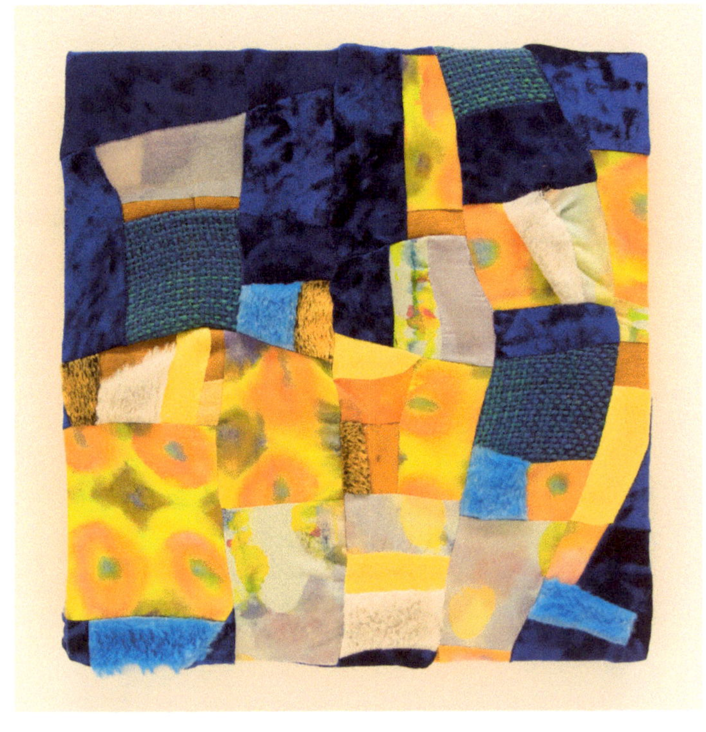

Isabelle O'Donnell
Rumble, 2017
Dye, green tea, fabric paint,
cotton fabric, velour, faux fur,
hand woven wool, canvas, 12 x 12in.

Friend of The Artist

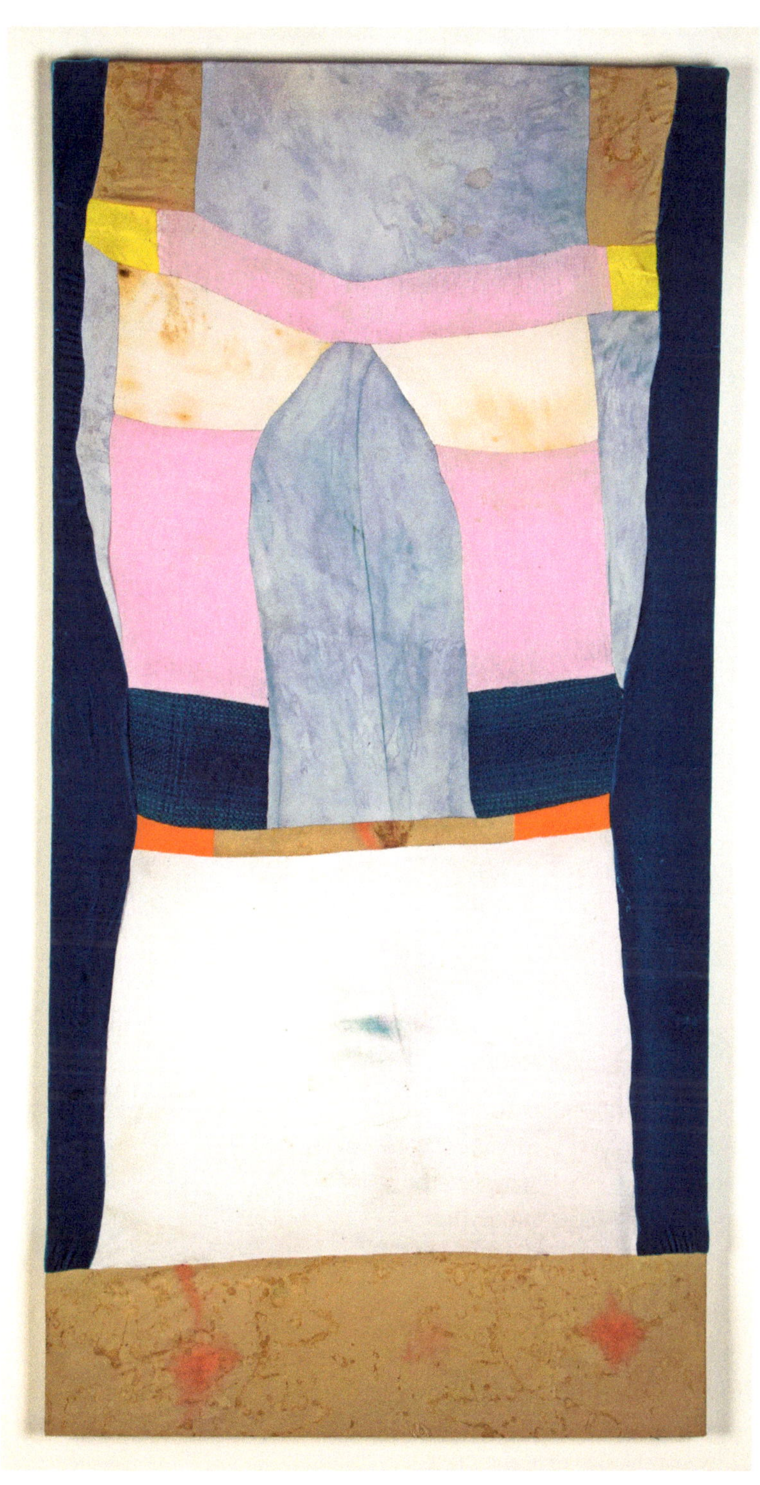

Isabelle O'Donnell
Afternoon Slumber, 2017
Red cabbage, vinegar, baking soda, salt, coffee,
food coloring, glue, cotton fabric, hand-loomed
wool weaving, velour, 30 x 60 in.

Leah Oates

Brooklyn, New York   leahoates.com

"The world thus appears to be a complicated tissue of events in which connections of different kinds alternate, overlap or combine and thereby determine the texture of the whole. All phenomena are processes, connections, all is in flux, and at moments this flux is visible."
Peter Matthiessen, *The Snow Leopard*

The Transitory Space series deals with urban and natural locations that are transforming due to the passage of time, altered natural conditions, and a continual human imprint. In everyone and in everything there are daily changes and this series articulates fluctuation in the photographic image and captures movement through time and space.

Transitory spaces have a messy human energy that is perpetually in the present yet continually altering. They are endlessly interesting, alive places where there is a great deal of beauty and fragility. They are temporary monuments to the ephemeral nature of existence.

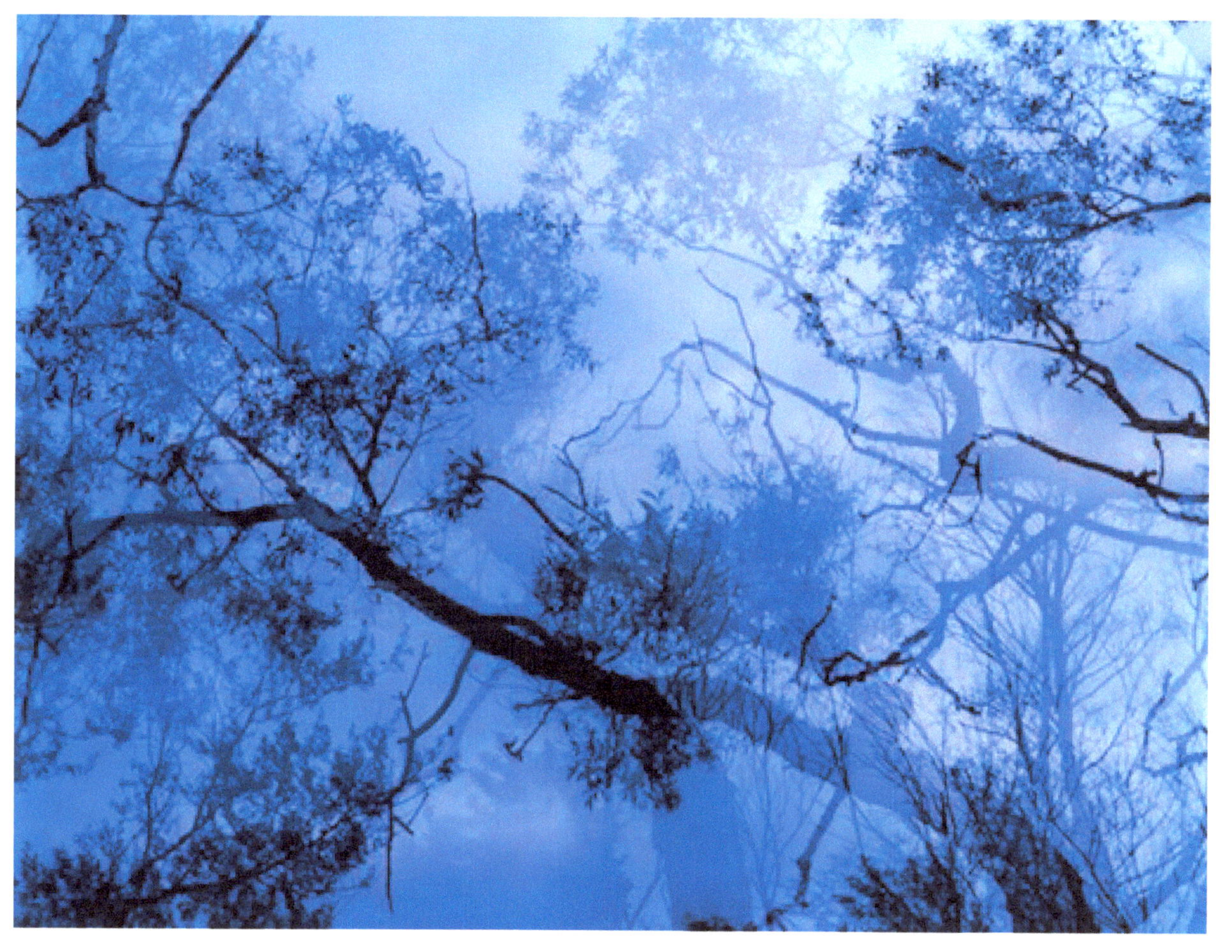

Leah Oates
Transitory Space, Newfoundland, Canada,
Rene Mill 11, 2008-2009
Color photography,
Image 11 x 16 in., Framed 16 x 20 in.

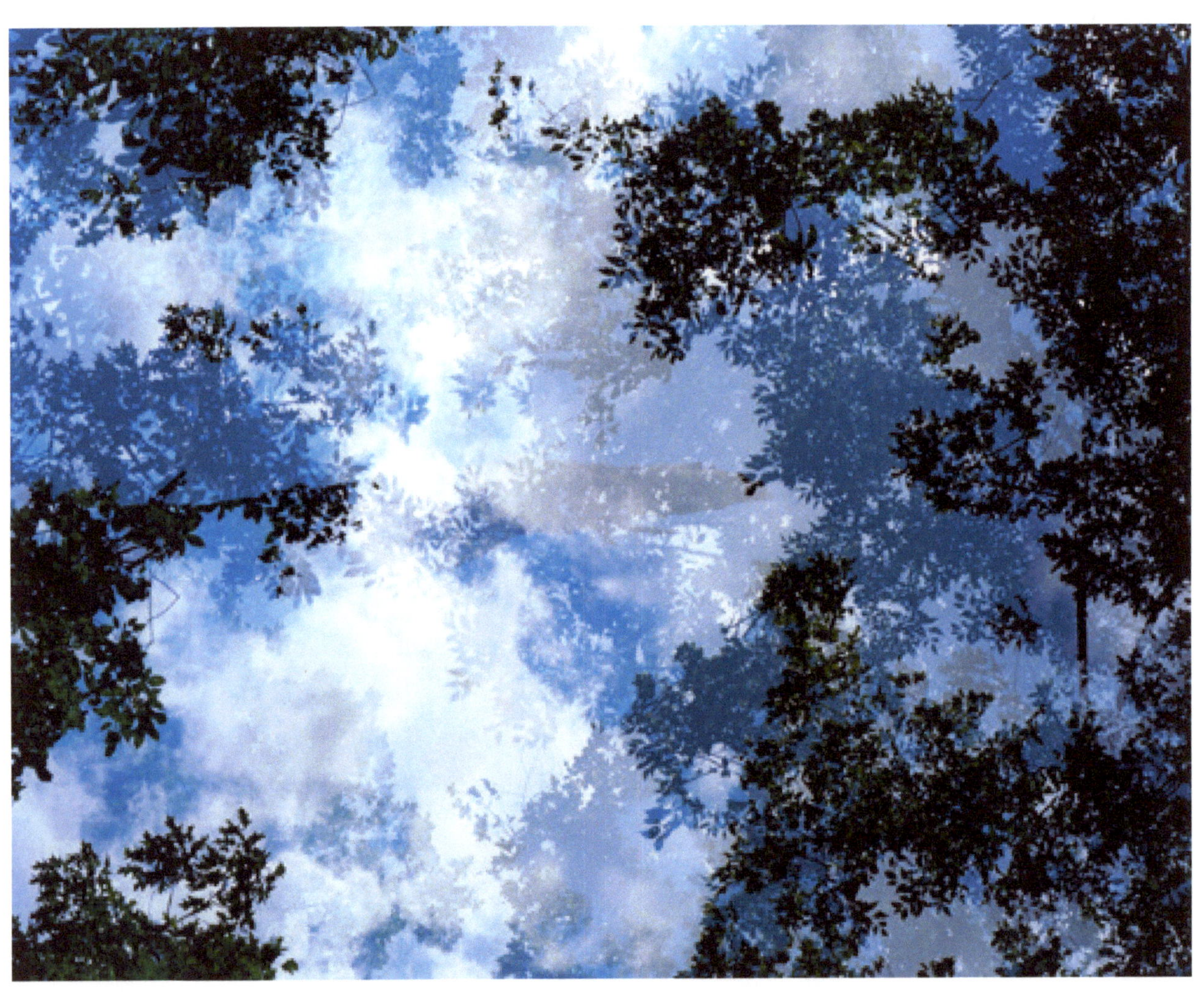

Leah Oates
Transitory Space, Brooklyn, Prospect
Park, Blue Tree Look Up #21, 2013-2014
Color Photography,
Image 11 x 16 in., Framed 16 x 20 in.

Friend of The Artist

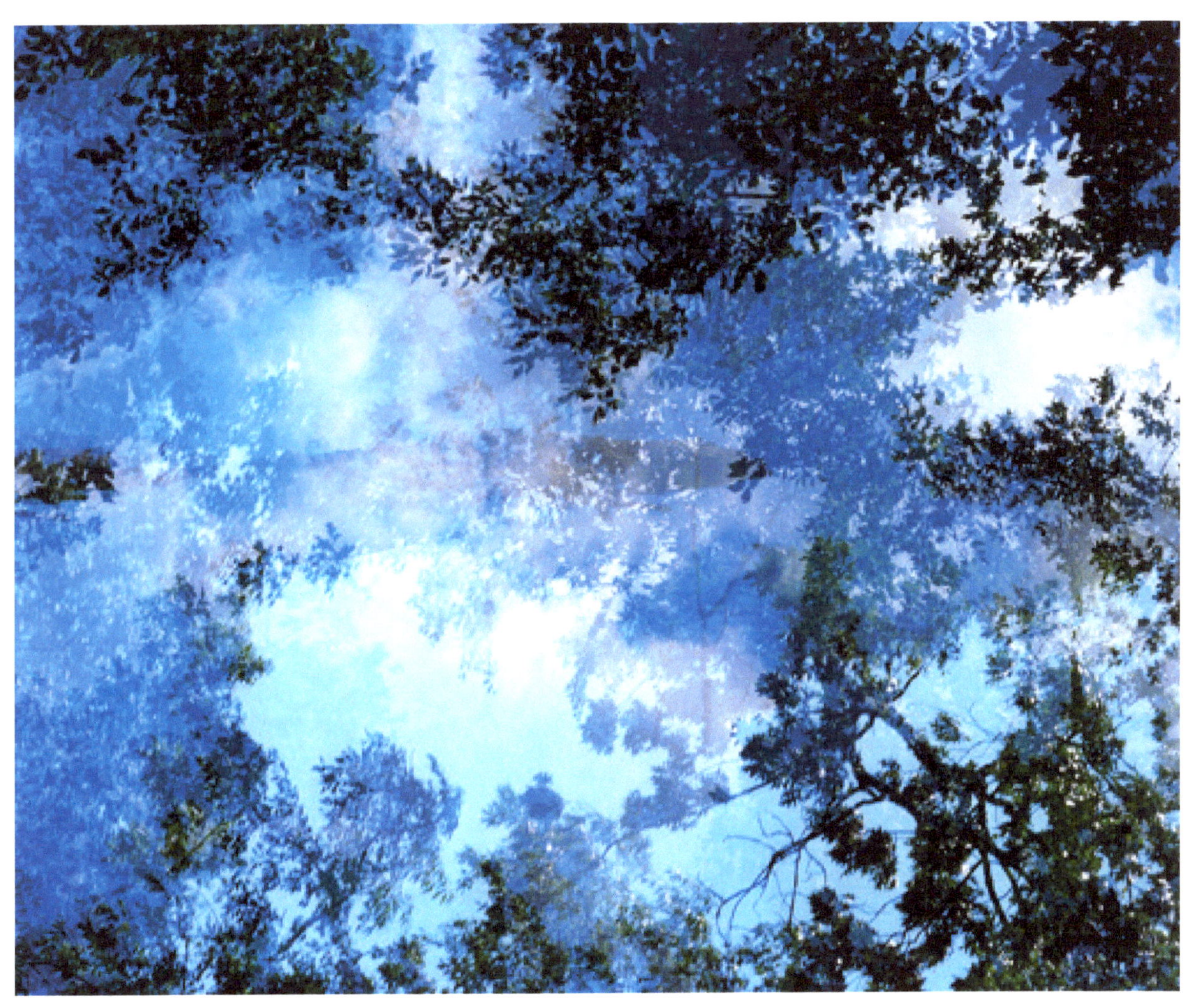

Leah Oates
Transitory Space, Brooklyn, Prospect
Park, Blue Tree Look Up #23, 2013-2014
Color Photography,
image 11 x 16 in., Framed 16 x 20 in.

Norton Pease

Havre, Montana   nortonpease.com

S. Norton Pease was born in Peoria, IL in 1972 and received his MFA from Washington University, St. Louis in 1999. His multilayered figurative portrayals synthesize different traditions and genres, while playing with perceptions of identity and social order. His paintings are an accumulation of various stylistic influences which address political and social issues.

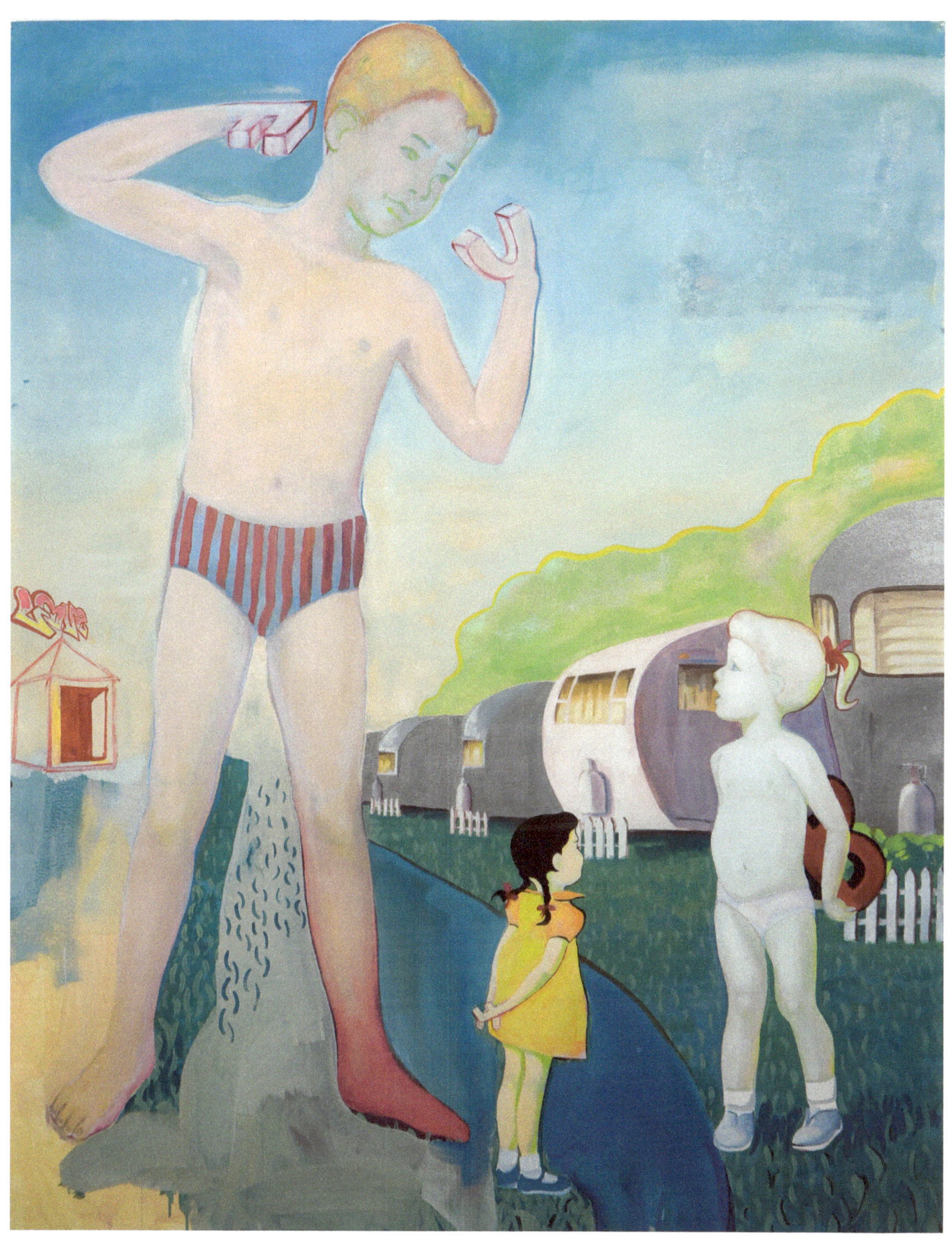

Norton Pease
[sic], 2012
Oil and enamel on paper,
54 x 40.5 in.

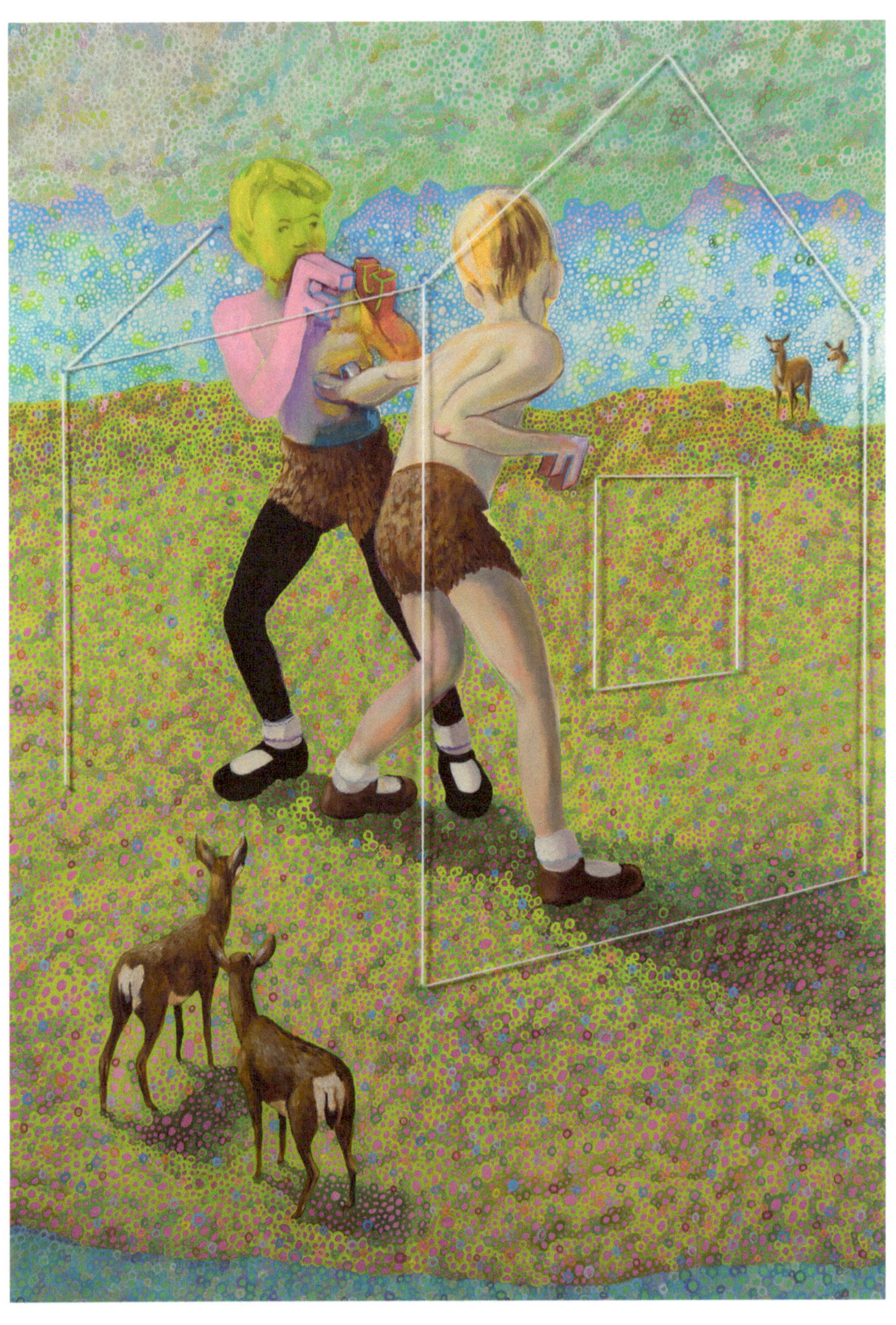

Norton Pease
Foofoo, 2016
Oil, yarn & pushpins on paper,
51 x 35.5 in.

Friend of The Artist

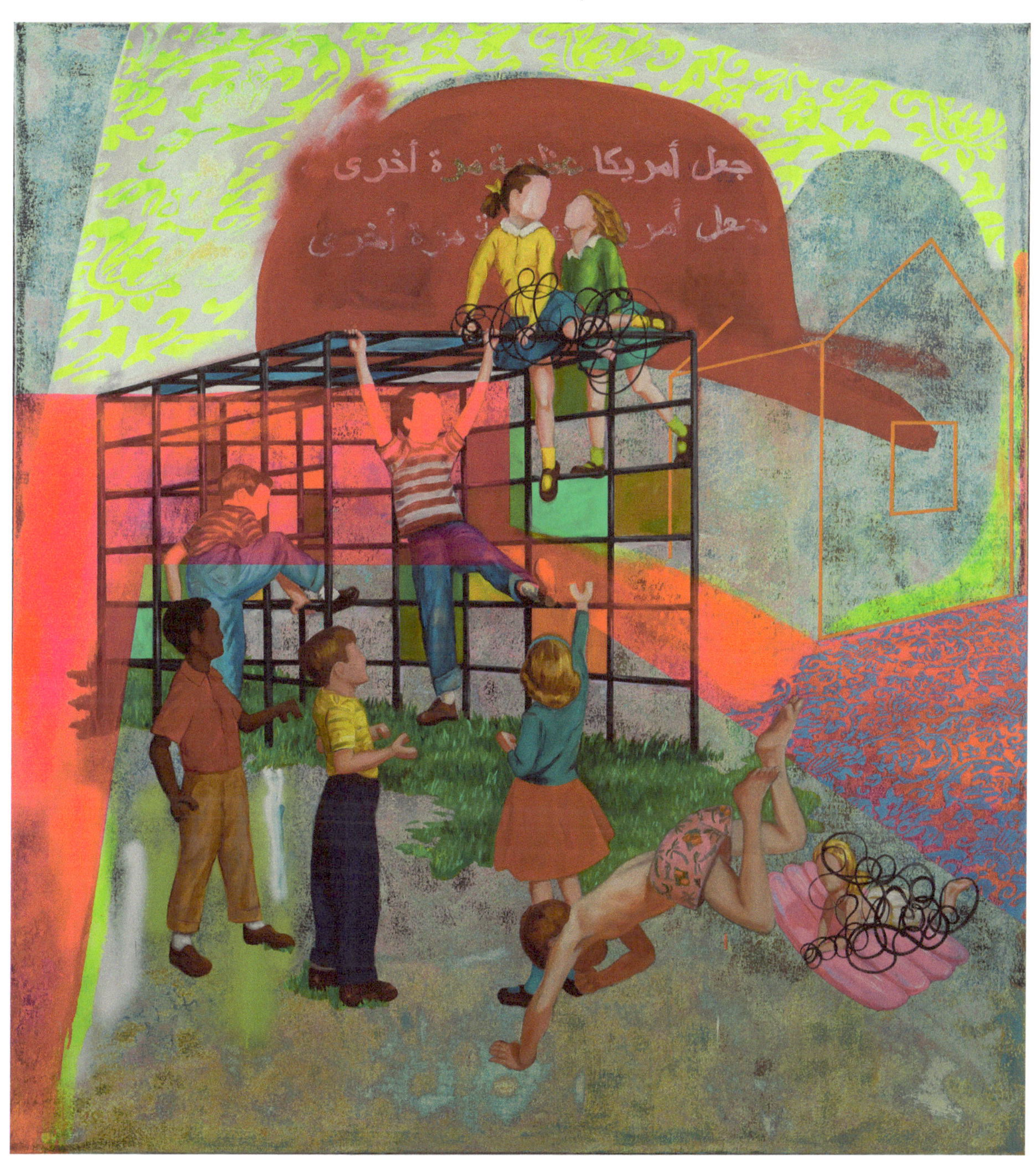

Norton Pease
MAGA (I Know Words, I Have The Best Words), 2017
Oil, enamel & glitter on canvas,
70 x 64 In.

Cara Roberts

Lisburn, Northern Ireland   cararoberts.co.uk

My art practice is currently concerned with the physicalities of mental state and psychological disorder—mostly focusing on self experience, but also exploring how to provoke this in others.

Increased heart rate, heavy chest, tension headaches, dizziness, shaking, shortness of breath, insomnia, hot flashes; are all physical symptoms of an anxiety disorder. I have had this since I was young, and it's what I use to inform my work.

I try to create an atmosphere of tension and apprehension using sculptural installation, video, and performance—mostly focusing on using my own body through acts of physical endurance, along with different materials to convey the symptoms I experience.

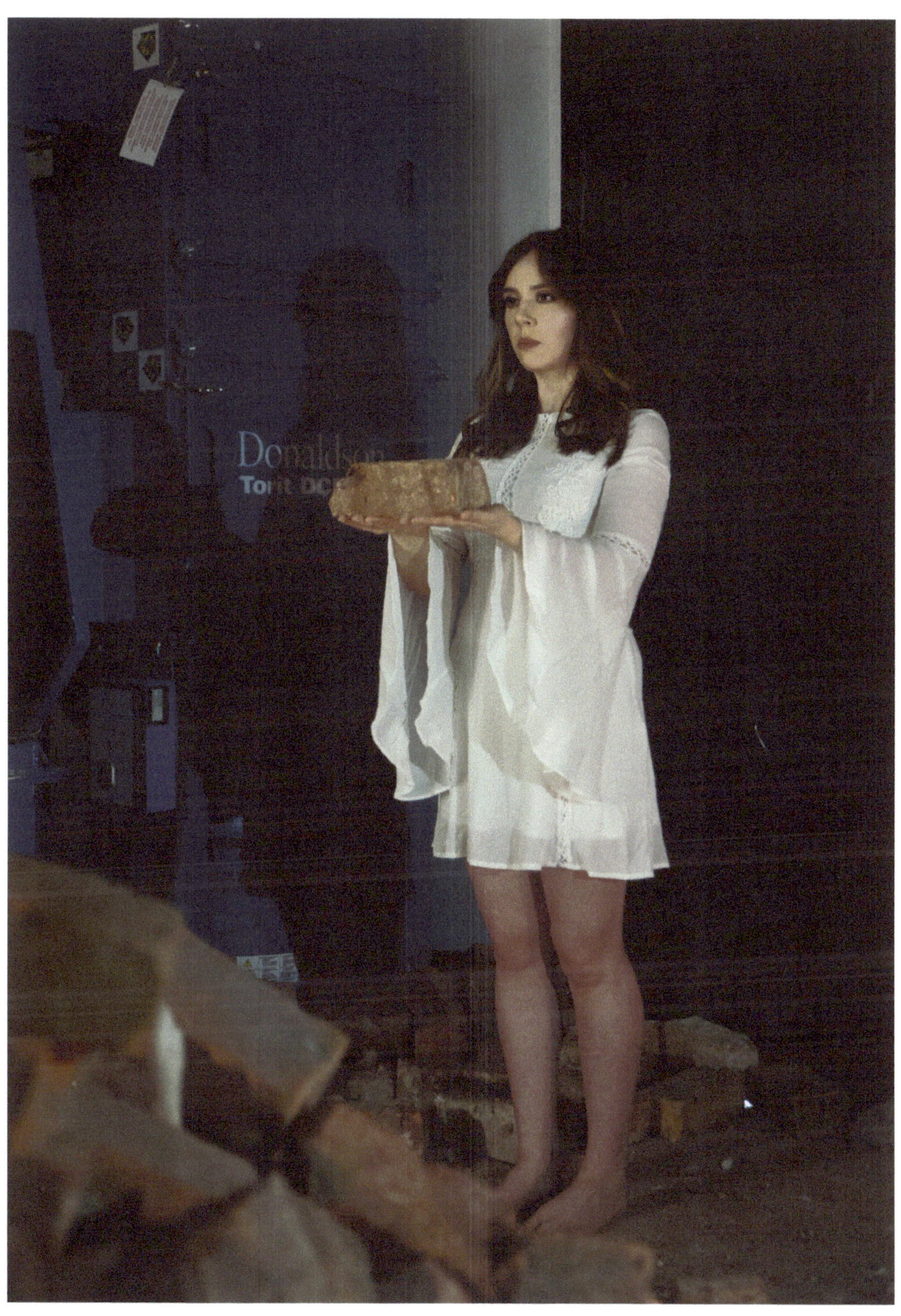

Cara Roberts
Headspace – Performance, 2017
Sculptural installation with video and performance,
Deminsions variable

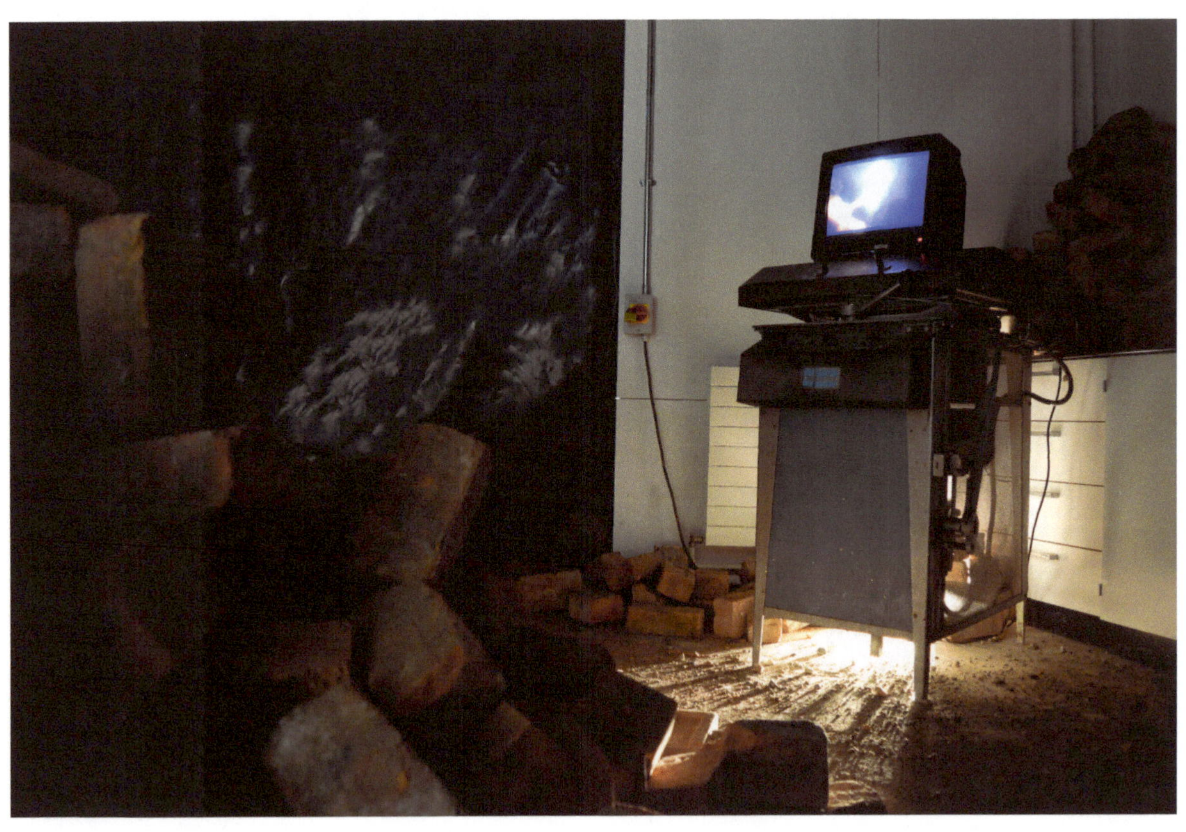

Cara Roberts
Headspace – Hot Flash, 2017
Sculptural installation with video and
performance,
Deminsions variable

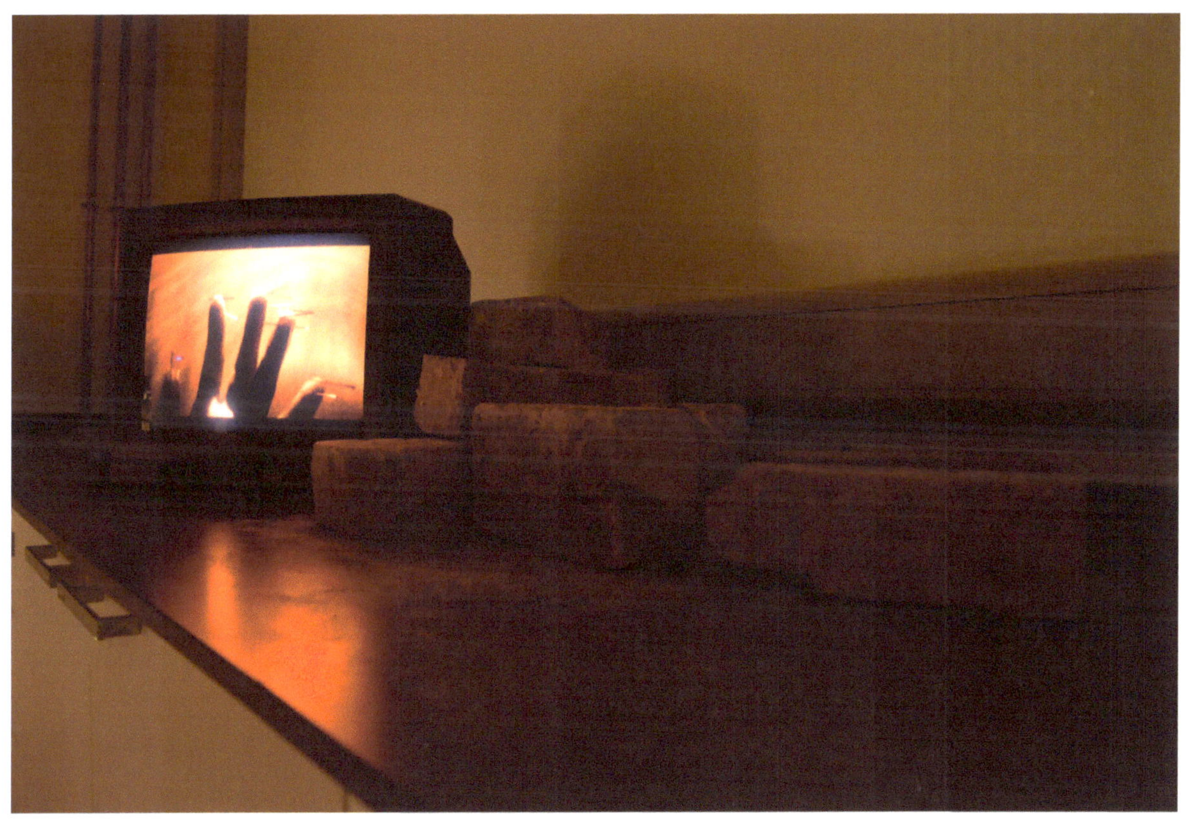

Cara Roberts
Headspace – Pins and Needles, 2017
Sculptural installation with video and
performance,
Deminsions variable

Ekaterina Vanovskaya

Philadelphia, Pennsylvania   vanovskaya.com

Pale, distressed figures inhabit my large-scale oil paintings. There are several repeating themes in the paintings: loneliness, nostalgia, longing, melancholia, and a search for a sense of place. There are often figures depicted doing mundane tasks, or caught in a state of hesitation or fear, in forlorn atmospheres. A specific emotional longing translates into a painting. I was born and spent my childhood in St. Petersburg, Russia and memorable childhood experiences frame the core of my work. These memories symbolize isolated experiences and therefore have a strong emotional impact. I no longer occupy the physical places and they do not exist in the same state. All is imagined.

How does our past impact our emotions, responses and ways of being? These perceptions of our childhood inevitably define the way we live our lives today. Painting starts to serve as reconciliation with the self. It is as if I am painting about a secret that nobody else knows.

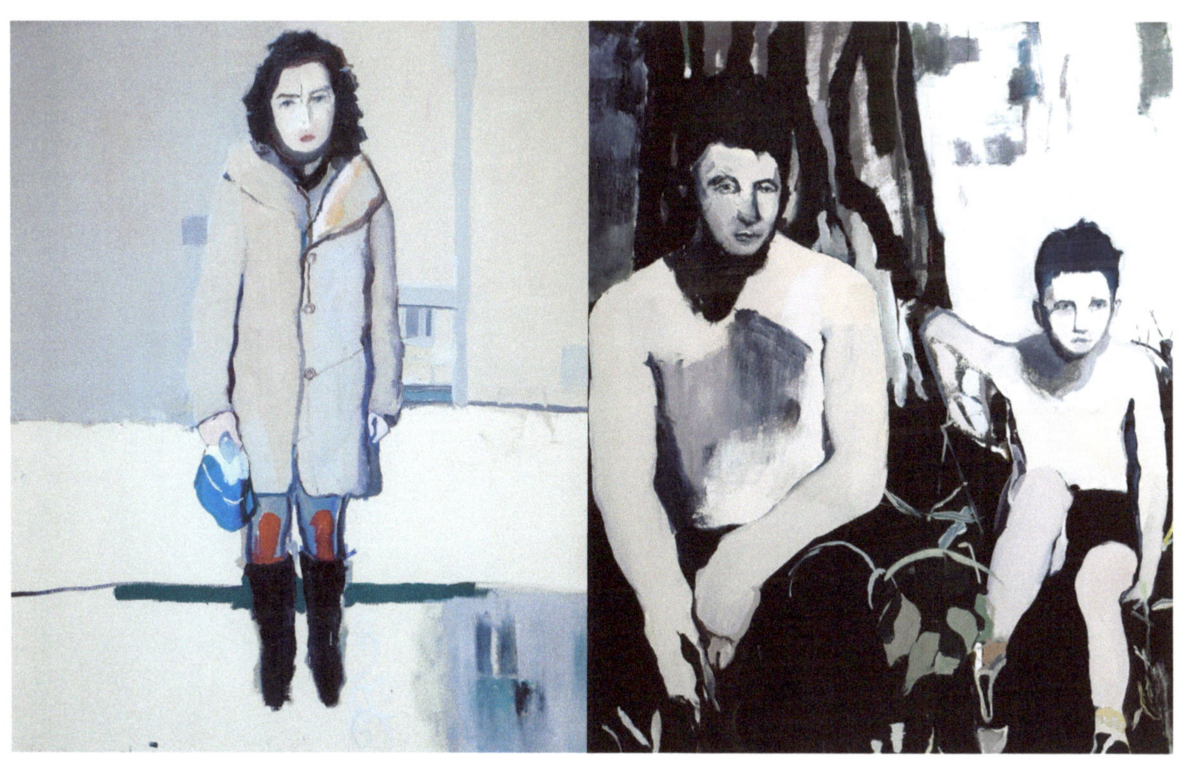

Ekaterina Vanovskaya
Things That Were, 2017
Oil on canvas, diptych,
36 x 60 in.
(each panel 36 x 30 in.)

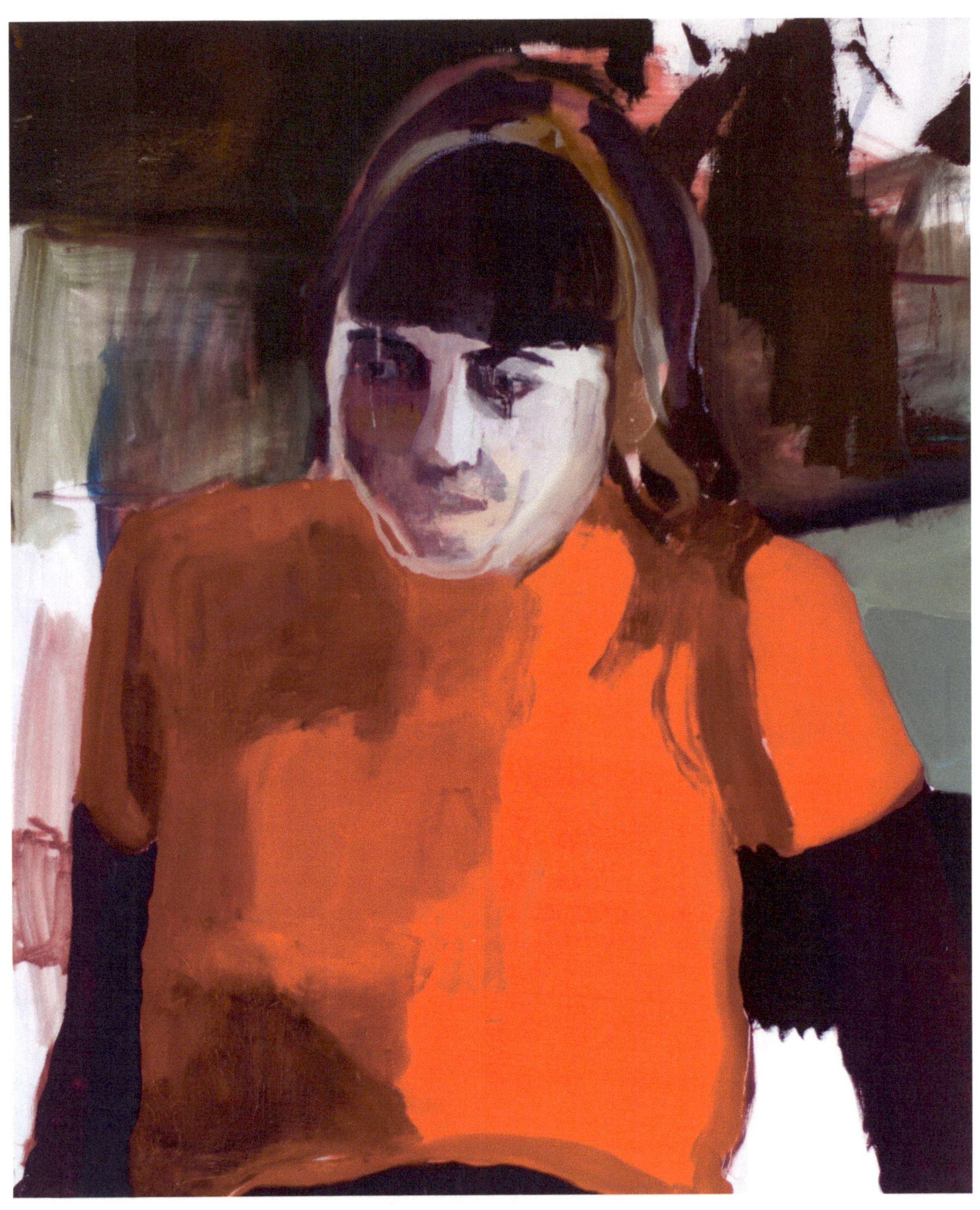

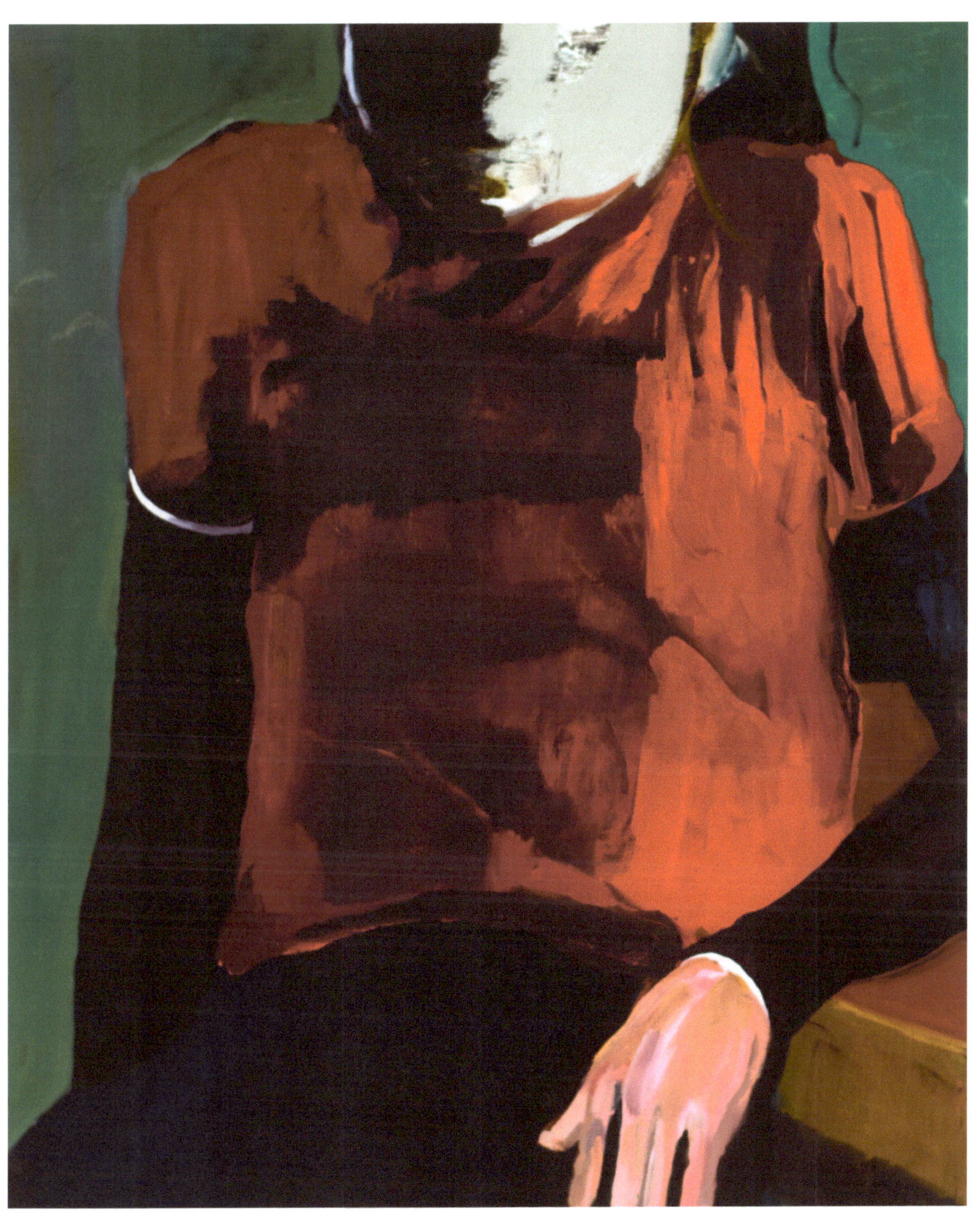

Ekaterina Vanovskaya
Red Sweater, 2017
Oil on Linen,
36 x 42 in.

Anna Wehrwein
Knoxville, Tennessee   annawehrwein.com

"The alternative is the thrill that comes from leaving the past behind without rejecting it, transcending outworn or oppressive forms, or daring to break normal pleasurable expectations in order to conceive a new language of desire."

– Laura Mulvey, *Visual Pleasure and Narrative Cinema*

This room is probably familiar. We've been here before—Ingres' bathhouse, Cassatt's blue chair, Matisse's red studio—rectangles (rooms and pictures) filled with women. And while these rooms may be outworn and oppressive, what with their heavy drapes and plush rugs (I do quite like the pattern), my desire is not to leave, but to radically rearrange.

I make paintings and drawings that reimagine the domestic space as a site of creative action and communal agency. Within the established settings of home and garden, the women in the paintings—all of them friends and fellow artists—engage in manual and immersive tasks. They cut each other's hair, give each other tattoos, and repot houseplants. These are scenes that, while based on real events, appear fictive, even utopian. Through the limited aperture of cinematic lens and painting precedent, intimate gestures and mise-en-scène may be interpreted as zones of maternal nurturing or eroticism. But this limited reading of madonna or harem is not so much inaccurate as unsatisfying. The figures themselves are not particularly concerned with how they are being looked at or who is looking at them. Instead, they are absorbed in drawing, watching, and listening—in what they are looking at.

CONTINUED ON PAGE 96 →

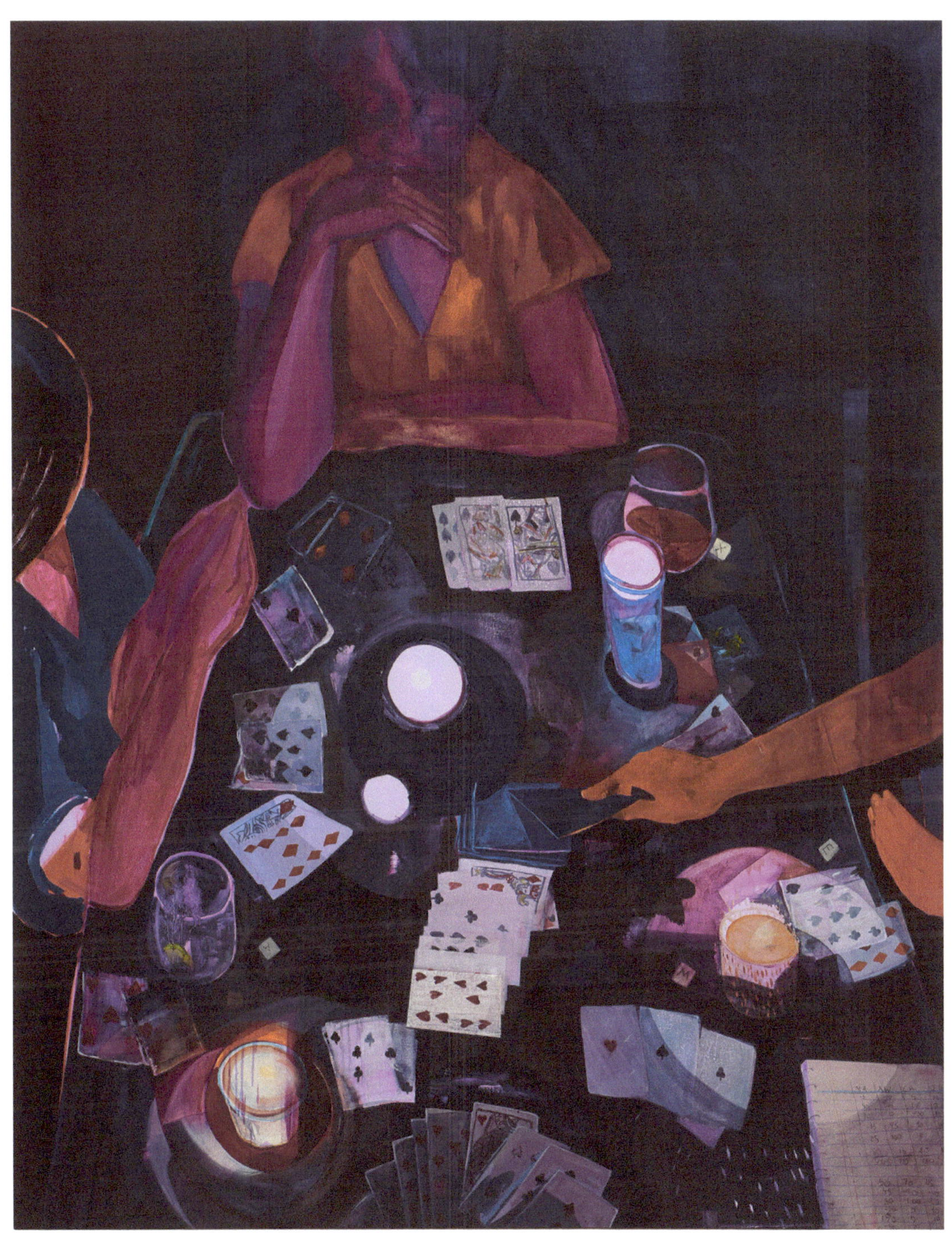

Anna Wehrwein
Power Outage, 2017
Oil on canvas, 60 x 48 in.

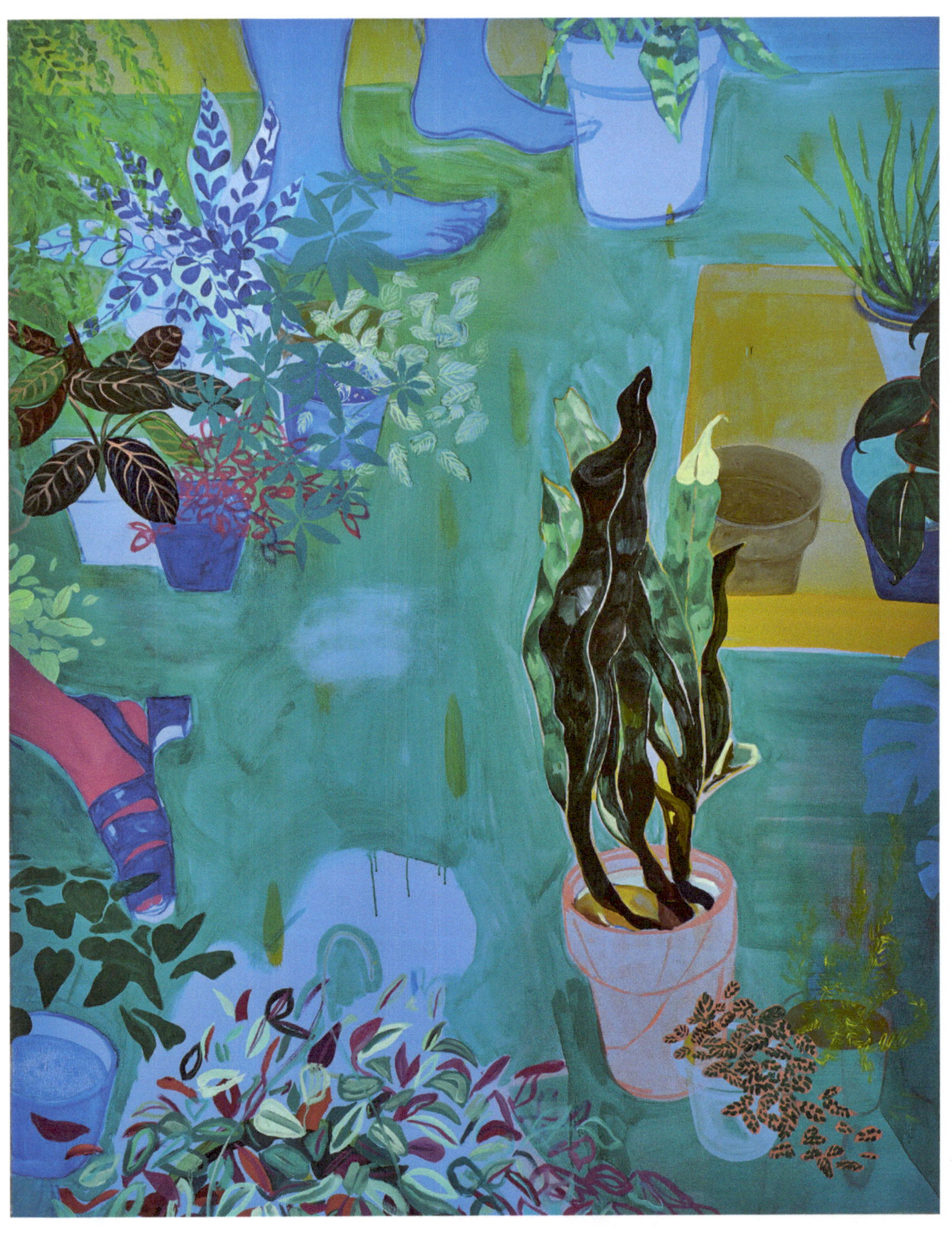

Anna Wehrwein
Replanted (by falling asleep she
becomes a plant), 2016
Oil on canvas, 60 x 48 in.

Friend of The Artist

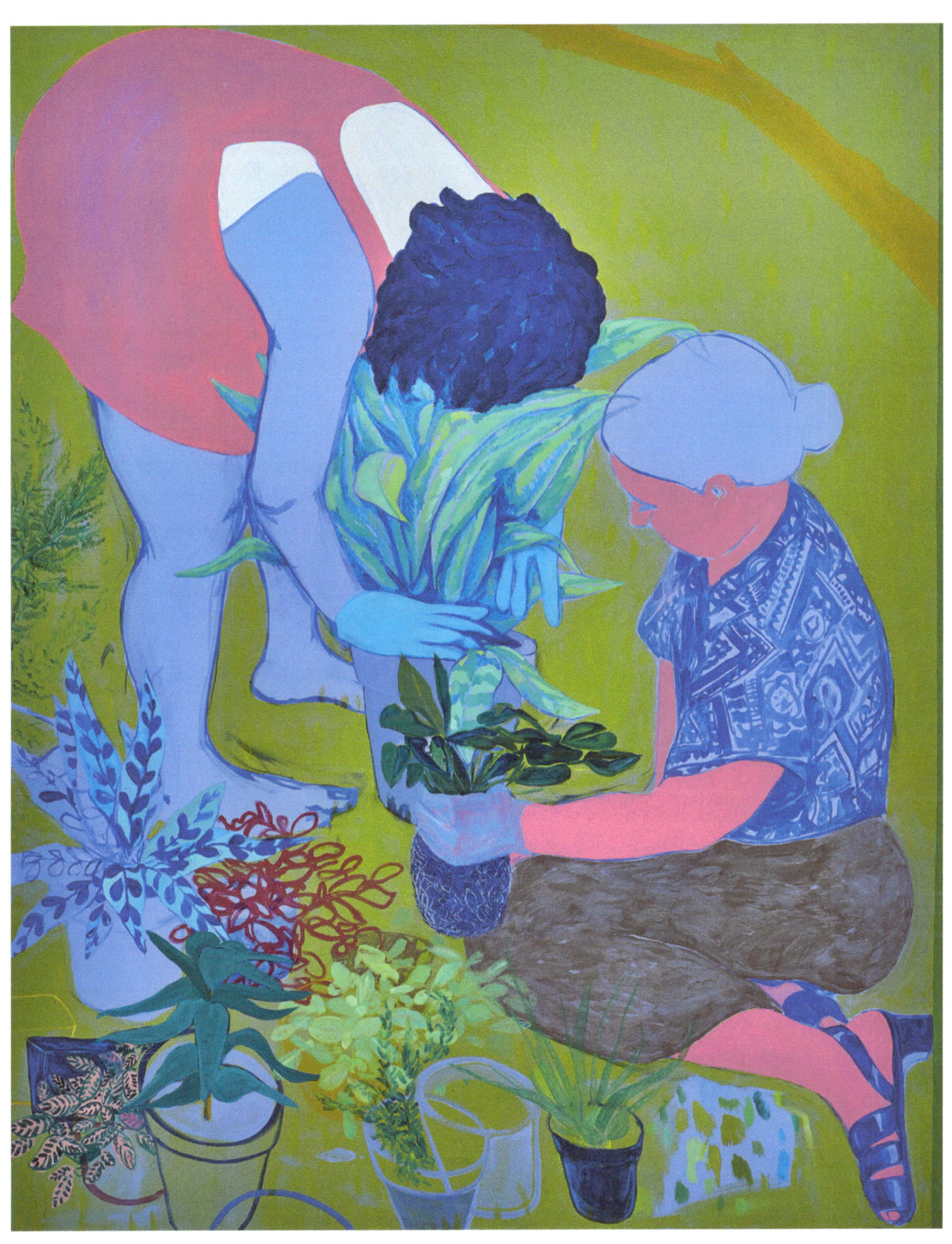

Anna Wehrwein
The Replanters, 2016
Oil on canvas,
60 x 48 in.

Artist Statements Continued

Miya Ando Ando's work has been exhibited extensively throughout the world, including a show curated by Guggenheim curator Nat Trotman, the Queens Museum, the De Saisset Museum, The Second Bronx Biennial at the Bronx Museum, The Hermitage Museum, The Museum of Contemporary Art Santa Barbara satellite space, The Attleboro Arts Museum, The Museum of Byzantine Culture, The Newhouse Center for Contemporary Art and the Worcester Museum. Miya's public commissions include projects in South Korea, Berlin, London, Puerto Rico, New York and California. Her work appears in many important public and private collections and she is the recipient of the Pollock Krasner Foundation Grant in 2012, the Thanatopolis Special Artist Award and Public Outdoor Commission Winner and Puffin Foundation Grant winner. A recent critics' picks of ARTFORUM, Ando received her Bachelor of Science Magna Cum Laude in East Asian Studies at UC Berkeley and continued her studies at Yale University, in addition to serving as an apprentice to a master metal smith in Japan. Miya's large scale artwork "Emptiness The Sky" (Shou Sugi Ban) is featured in "Frontiers Reimagined" exhibition in the 56th Venice Biennale. Most recently she was commissioned by The Philip Johnson Glass House to create a sculpture, "Shizen" (Nature) "Kumo" (Cloud) and her work has been acquired for the permanent contemporary collection by The Los Angeles County Art Museum (LACMA).

Lauren Christlieb Sifting through my Great Grandmother's things that my grandfather had kept, I found a card that she'd written to my father, "It's hard to believe you're 20!" written in her proper cursive and now dated handwriting. The envelope was addressed to the same house I grew up in. We were connected across decades, and that's what drew me in, that familiarity. Rather than recreate the card or sentiment inside, I chose to recreate and screen-print the envelope larger than life.

Letters are often thrown in a box and forgotten about. One minute they communicate unbridled passion and the next they're smashed in the back of a junk drawer. Written to her mother, my great grandmother expressed her stress with money: "It seems my money just goes. I guess I have to learn how to save. We all have to learn." This is certainly something I can relate to, as with so many of the letters I found. By enlarging them to twice their original size, I am giving them a second life. I chose to isolate sentences that resonated with me in various ways, whether via their irony, humor, or something that resonated with me on a personal level or even simply what I remembered from reading through them the first time. By presenting only these fragments, I also emphasize selective memory and the process of remembering in general.

Paper is such an important medium in storytelling and another way it is used in After He Passed is in the recreation of teacups with cardboard and papier-mâché. I used obituaries from some of my grandfather's old newspapers for the papier-mâché. To paint them,

I studied the original cups for fifteen minutes and then painted what I could remember of the original filigree. The teacups are not something I remember well. I remember them in china cabinets, too high for my little hands to reach. In my memory, we did not use them. They weren't to be touched; they were displayed high up, in a glass cabinet, only to be admired. Recreating these cups out of paper, something that is not breakable, has allowed me to create a completely new and different experience than the one I had as a child.

My great grandmother's sunflower painting was my first encounter with a work of art. As a child I loved looking at it and I feel it symbolizes and perhaps even catalyzed the beginning of my career in art making. Great Grandmother was a Sunday painter who painted because she loved to. It needed to be big because it looms so large in my memory and was instrumental in how I chose to lead my life.

After He Passed aims to underscore the power of memory. Specifically, it recreates one of my earliest memories and suggests a deeply rooted initiation into the world of art making. Through visual, tactile, and even taste-induced cues, I have accessed my own early memories in the viewer as well. Such memories offer connectivity to the past, and hint at who we are today.

Megan St. Clair I make artwork when it is emotionally easy and when it is emotionally muddy and complicated because it is all relevant. I think of the artwork as poetic and scientific gestures to offer up to myself as an opportunity to reflect on my own personal narrative of emotional vulnerability. Our intimate failures and successes bleed into our memories in very unique and lasting ways. Emotional vulnerability involves a group dynamic–at least a group of two. The closest people we hold on to have the potential to build us or to diminish us.

Peter Hiatt By cooperating in this directed movement, users of a retail store enter into a social contract, implicitly agreeing to its rules for their own perceived benefit. This directing of movement extends to the parking lot around a retail store. Many of these retail centers have a ditch along their perimeter that directs the flow of water, while simultaneously acting as an implied barrier. Trees grow dense and high, signifying that they are not to be breached; that this is the edge of the designated space for people and vehicles. Without necessarily realizing it, most people understand and agree to these terms. These ditches, and the retail centers they border, have become so familiar that people do not notice them, or think critically about the implications of their existence. I decided to break the social contract of the retail park, and enter into these ditches.

Inside these ditches is a fascinating world. There is usually a slow-moving stream of water, surrounded by dense foliage. The trees form a canopy, which, combined with the density of the brush, completely encloses one in the space.

These places house the refuse of a consumer society, carried there by the flow of water. Plastic bags and bottles, aluminum cans, and pieces of concrete are strewn about.

The most striking objects are shopping carts, which become fascinating objects in this setting. Jutting out of the ground at odd angles, the bright color of their plastic baskets and logos create a strong contrast to the natural mud and brambles that surround them. They are in the midst of being swallowed by the earth; slowly being re-absorbed and disintegrated. Although signs of decomposition can be seen in the rusted metal of the carts, their bright plastic baskets look almost brand new. People dig these ditches and manage the growth around them, but what happens inside of them, away from human eyes, is random, messy nature. Evidence of society is present in the form of garbage, but these objects are dissociated from their practical applications, thus adding to the chaos. This a place that is as close as one's backyard, but it is shut out, because it is unpleasant to experience.

By making images from inside drain ditches near retail centers, I am raising consciousness about how people are conditioned to view the world around them. A child is curious about everything, because they recognize nothing as normal; everything is new and interesting. Adults grow used to certain aspects of their lives, such as retail stores, which they must look at and interact with frequently in order to participate in society. As they grow used to things, they cease to notice them, and think critically about them. This intellectual invisibility is a source great power for institutions, which often perpetuate themselves by avoiding scrutiny. My goal with all of my work, and with this series in particular, is to force the viewer to look at and contemplate the banal things of everyday life. By doing this, I am encouraging a sense of skepticism and critical thinking about the world. I want people to be able to recognize absurdities in the world, even if they have existed all of their life. This sense of skepticism should cause one to question the wisdom of contemporary society's relationship with the land., while playing with perceptions of identity and social order. His paintings are an accumulation of various stylistic influences which address political and social issues.

Justin Korver The nail is passive, acted on, pounded. However, the tools in The Expressive Mark & Other Ideas I Stole From Painting have been stripped of their usefulness. They have been made passive, decorative, pretty by the application of paint. Like the abstract expressionists that attempted to make painting into an action but failed to do so. While miles of canvas and gallons of paint were expended in the pursuit of painting as an action; I think ultimately the history of paintings as useless, beautiful surfaces has persisted. It's the conflict between the usefulness of tools and the uselessness of paintings that provides the energising conflict of my work. It also seems to be an apt metaphor for the traditional conflict between notions of masculinity and femininity.

Artist Statements Continued

ISABELLE O'DONNELL Repetition and time play greatly into my practice, and many of the processes I utilize in my work are intimately connected to domesticity and the rhythms of daily life. I feel a close connection between my quotidian and art making activities as much of my making process occurs in the home.

My use of these techniques and processes of working connects to feminist work theory surrounding contemporary craft culture, and a reshaping of what was considered 'women's work' or home labour. The influx of working women and people of all genders taking up crafts such as knitting, sewing, and weaving publicizes and recontextualizes practices traditionally associated with the home and domesticity. The incorporation of these practices into the fine arts adds a different level of recognition and value to what was historically often a hidden labor, recontextualizing it as the work of the artist.

While my work looks to historical and contemporary artists, much of my art practice draws from my personal history and my educational experiences as a child. Growing up, my parents wanted a holistic, natural environment for me and my sister, and we were raised mostly without media, plastic toys, or foods with artificial coloring or flavoring. We were surrounded by natural materials such wool, cotton, and wood, and we participated in traditional craft processes such as sewing, knitting, natural dyeing and felting. As I have grown older, my aesthetic preferences and interests have developed in response and reaction to this upbringing. My pieces reflect this, incorporating saturated colors and synthetic materials into the sewing and dyeing processes I learned as a child.

Stemming from my interest in both traditional craft processes and sustainability I incorporate natural dyeing processes into my work. I am interested in examining our cultural entrenchment in commodity fetishism, while concurrently paying homage to hand crafts. I explore these dichotomies between crafting and consumerism in my work through contrasting hand dyed and woven textiles with repurposed synthetic materials, and acrylic paints and dyes. Using easily accessible foods and spices I dye yarn, fabric, and knit textiles which are then combined with repurposed fabrics, foams, and highly synthesized acrylic paints and mediums. The line between natural and artificial is a hazy one masked by advertising, preconceptions and separation from the manufacturing of the items we consume. These disparities and similarities present themselves in my work though my use of both natural foods and artificial food coloring in my dyeing processes, as well as plastics and textiles, contrasting and often combining the two. I am interested formally in the differences in material texture and saturation that arise, as well as the elements of accessibility, familiarity, time, and touch. The contemporary use of traditional craft processes is not just a reclamation of its traditions, but also a critical examination of mass production and consumer culture. Hand production personalizes an item, and disrupts the consume and discard cycles.

I situate myself as an artist within a growing lineage of contemporary painters whose work deals with painting's intrinsic connection to textiles and craft, exploring its conceptual implications regarding feminism and labour, process and material, and pattern and ornamentation. I seek to combine these varying processes, materials, and motifs in order to acknowledge their correlations and explore the histories and disciplines that have shaped my practice as a contemporary artist.

ANNA WEHERWEIN Creating a space for female viewers means more than simply not making women objects of desire, not turning them into an odalisque, an Ophelia, a houseplant. Nor does female authorship (mine included) necessarily create a progressive gaze.

Rather, the act of looking must accommodate multiple positions, with the opportunity to rotate the roles of object, subject, author, and audience. And yet this last vantage point, visual theorist Griselda Pollock writes, is both the most important and the most elusive. For "without that possibility" of the "female spectator," she warns, "women are denied a representation of desire."

And where is desire more palpable than in painting? What is more pleasurable than a surface covered in opaque pigment? A buttery shape, a dense field of pattern? These joys should never be denied. Yet within these surfaces and narratives, where might it be best (as Mulvey challenges us) to break from pleasurable expectations— to leave empty or cover over?

My only answer is to return to where the paintings begin, to the ultimate act of looking and watching—to drawing.

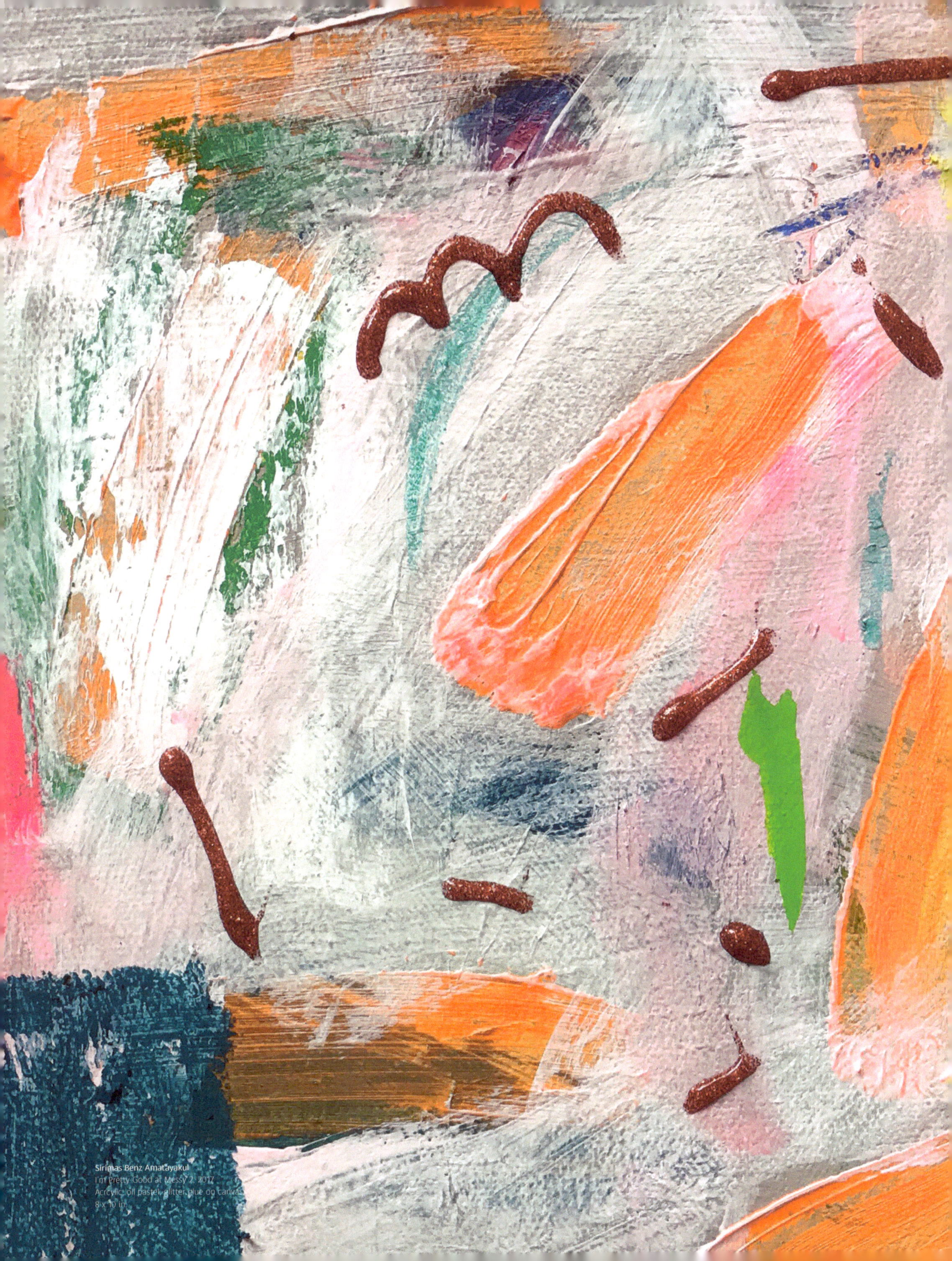

Sirimas Benz Amatayakul
I'm Pretty Good at Messy 2, 2017
Acrcylic, oil pastel, glitter glue on canvas
8 x 10 in.

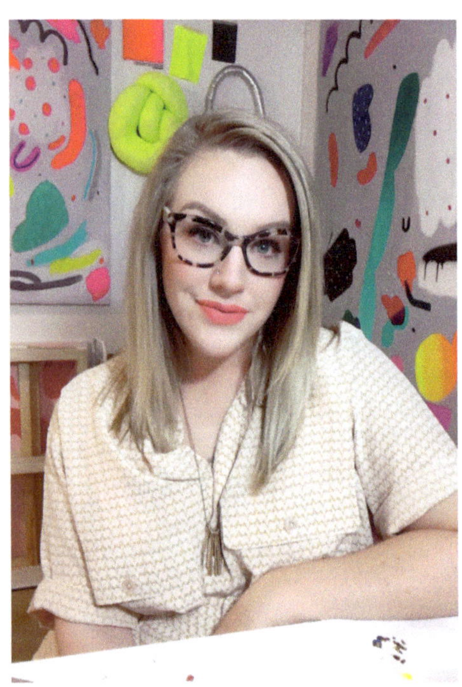

Samantha Keith *Founder, Fresh Contemporary*

Samantha Keith is the founder and curator of Fresh Contemporary Digest, a blog and platform for emerging and established artists. She will graduate with her BA in Studio Art from Fairmont State University in 2017, has exhibited throughout the U.S., as well as internationally in contemporary art publications.

Selected Works

Each of the following selected works present the viewer with a lushness and sense of heat, despite varying immensely in processes and product. Lisa Denyer's piece studies the interaction of positive and negative space with geometric shapes and organic brush strokes in a humid, steamy palette. Megan St. Clair's work has a powerful presence through the use of delicate contour line and mark making paired with more deliberate, objective forms. Sarah Boyts Yoder's use of palette and organic movement is wonderfully refreshing, pushing boundaries between deliberate and serendipitous composition.

Morgan Ward's work applies distinction between compositional elements in ways that, despite it's non objectivity, produces a nearly tangible sense of space and atmosphere. Each piece, through use of composition, form and colour, create a sense of lushness, teeming with heated movement and ardent colour.

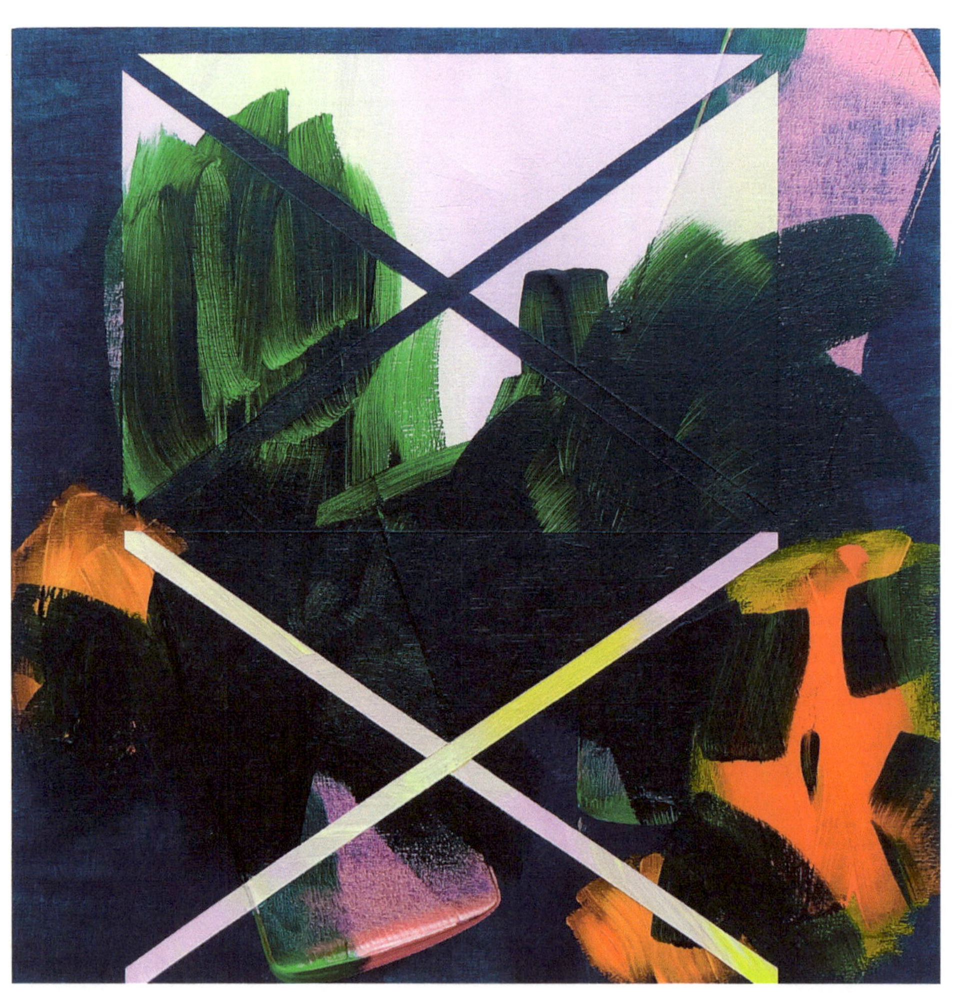

Lisa Denyer
Rousseau, 2017
Acrylic, emulsion and collage on panel

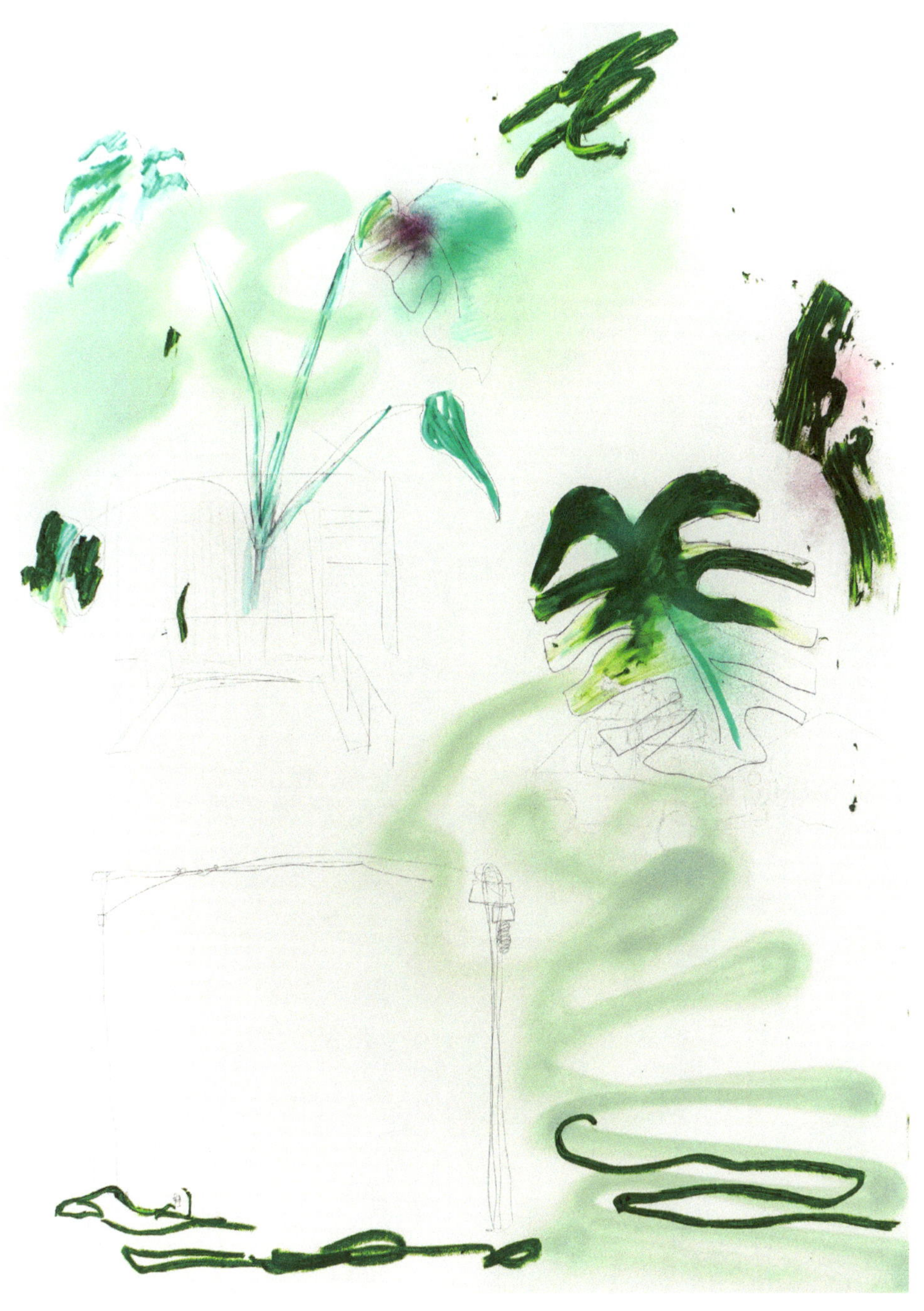

Megan St.Clair
Our First Plant, 2017
Oil and pencil on panel,
36 x 48 in.

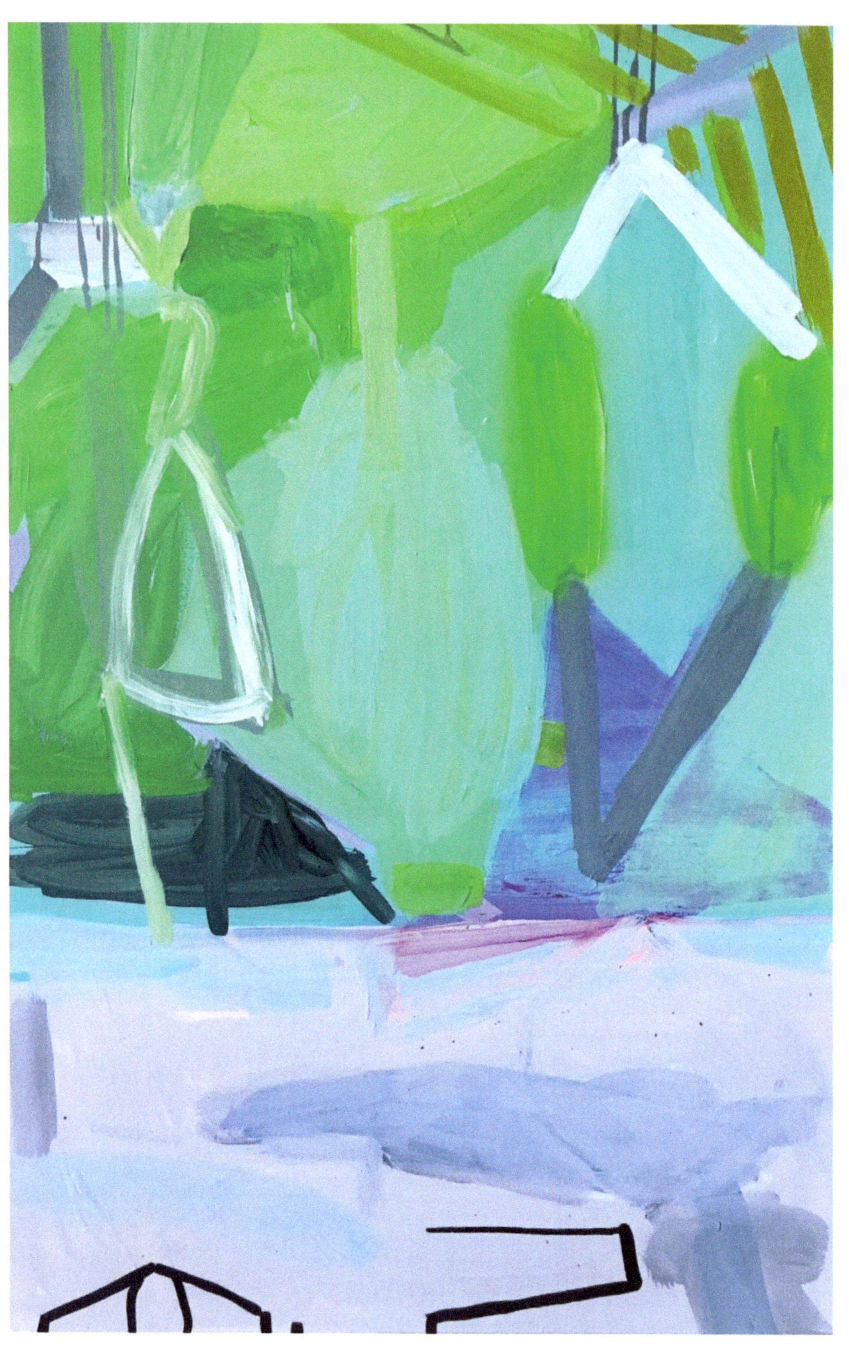

Sarah Boyts Yoder
The Jungle Over the Wall, 2017
Acrylic, ink, watercolor,
spray paint on canvas,
12 x 16 in.

Friend of The Artist

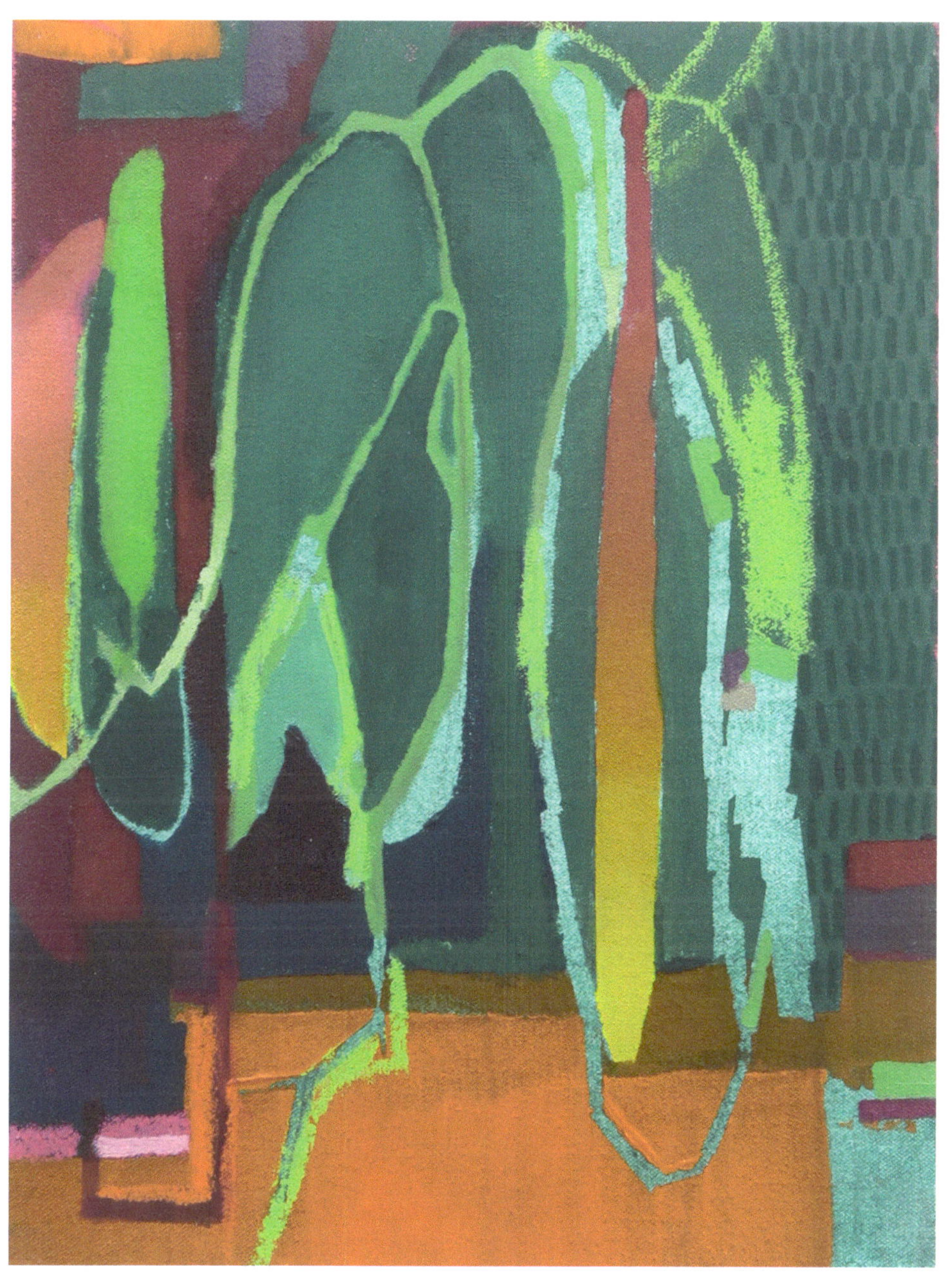

Morgan Ward
Untitled, 2017
Oil and oil pastel with acrylic wash on
canvas and board

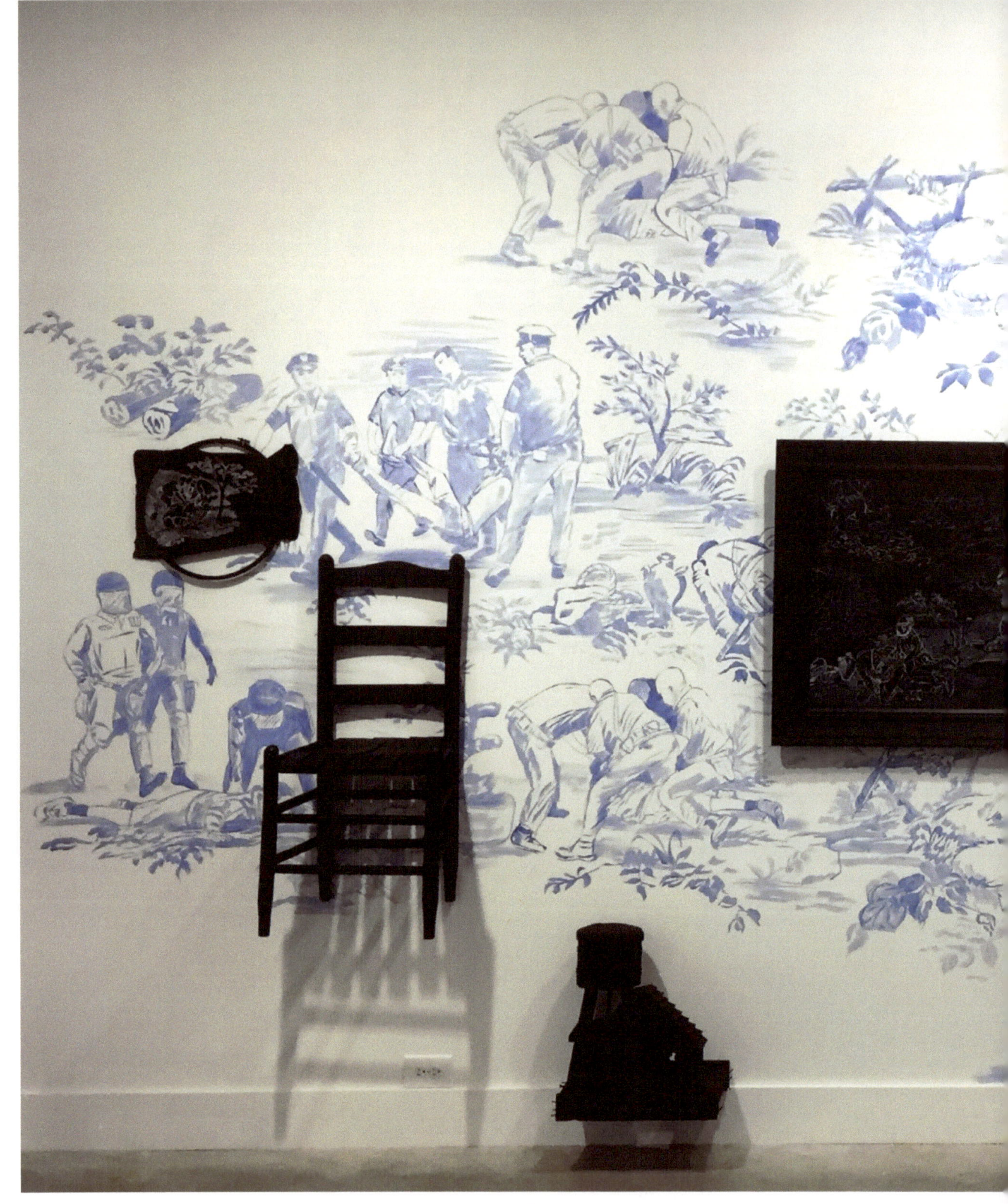

Hollis Hammonds
Domestic Brutality, 2017
Acrylic paint on wall, painted
objects &
chalk marker,
96 x 192 x 18 in.

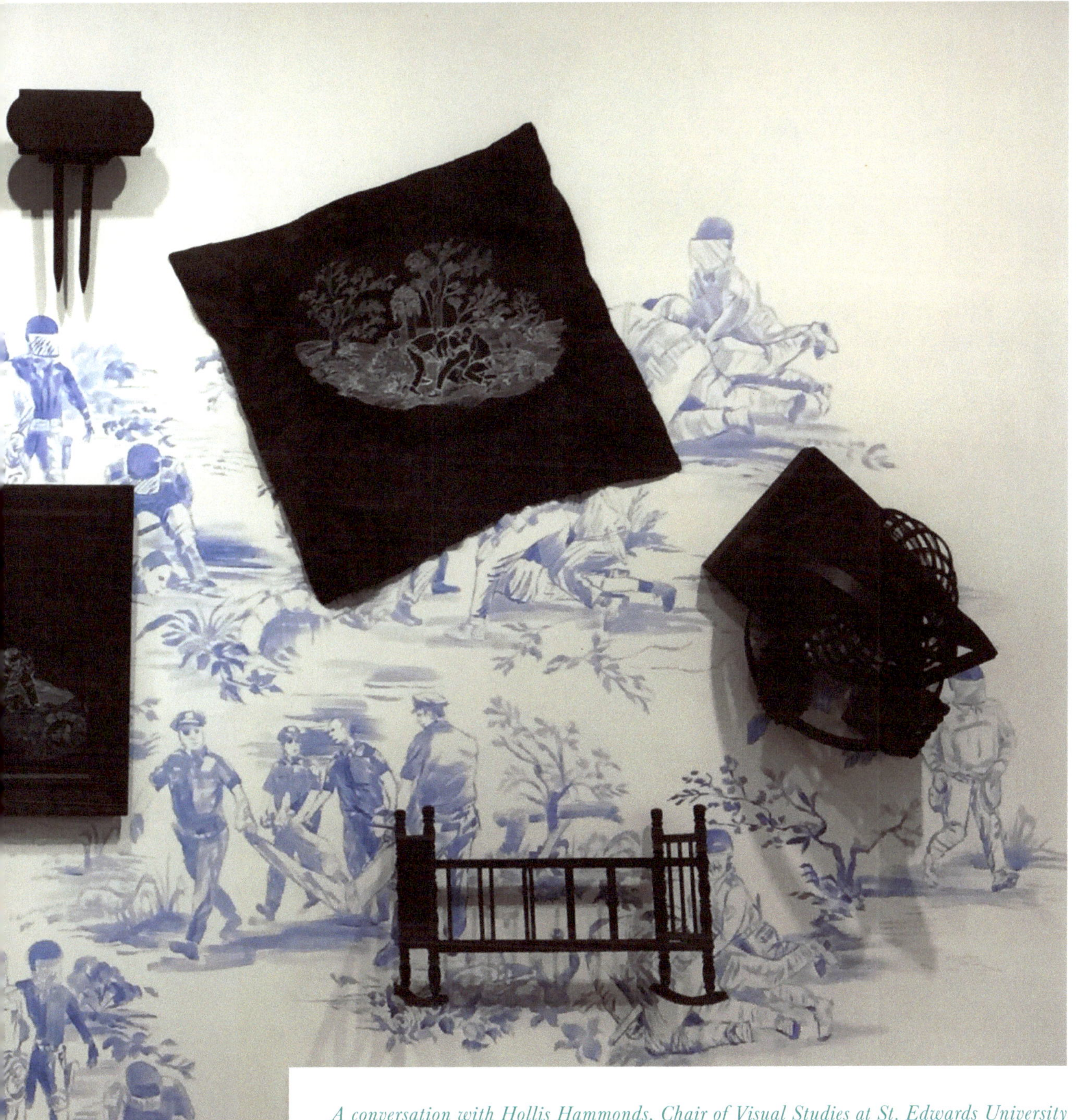

Works by Hollis Hammonds

Interviewed by Ty Bishop

& Justin Archer

Drawing on Beauty and Disaster

T: I want to start off by reading a quote from you. The quote is, "take a careful look at your surroundings and you will see that drawings are all around us." How does this relate to your drawing process?

H: I totally identify as a drawing person. Everything I do, even the sculptural work I'm making, I think about in the context of drawing. For me, drawing isn't as much about art making as it is thinking. Any work that I'm making, or even with how I'm engaging in the world, I feel like is in this weird, linear way. I'm always looking at line and thinking about movement. I think about all aspects of my life in the context of drawing. It's been what my main research has been about.

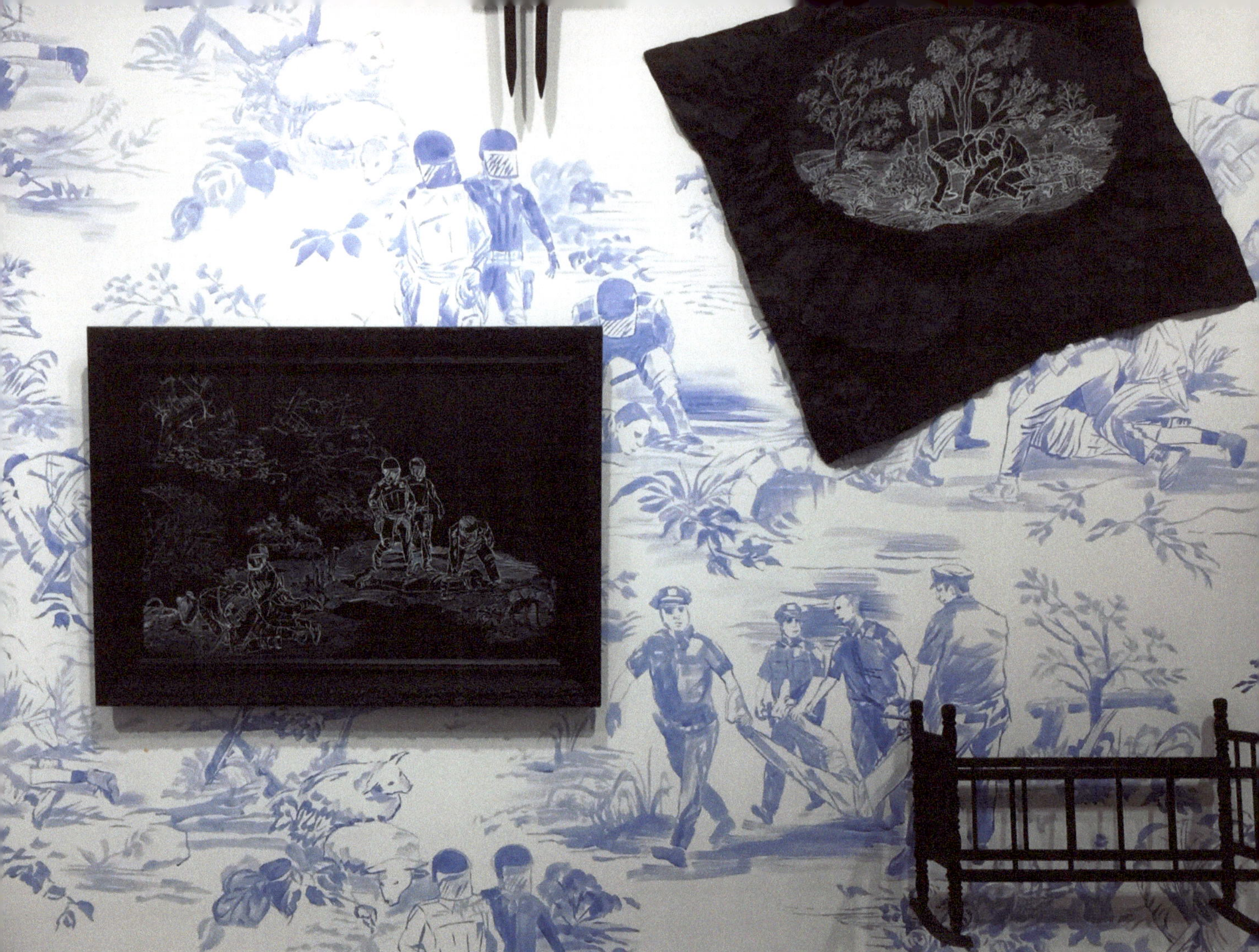

T: That reminds me of what Matisse said of his work. I was fascinated that he said something like "all of life is painting." For you, I think it's the same idea, but with drawing.

H: Totally.

J: A lot of your work is charcoal based. Why do you use charcoal? Is it because it is a thinking process?

H: It's funny because I mostly worked in charcoal when I was younger and came back to it in recent years. I did so more because of the identity of charcoal as a sort of burnt, black, charred thing that then can be manipulated. Because I work in all media, I'm not attached to a particular one. For particular works, charcoal is the thing that it has to be because of the nature of it. I'm really interested in it when I'm thinking about materials I'm using. It's the blackness and dirtiness of it. It's malleable, right? You can move it around and get volume. It's main characteristic for me is this burnt, blackness.

T: Which lends itself to your work.

H: I try to link it conceptually to what I'm doing instead of just the joy of working with it. Honestly, when I'm in the studio, I hate it so much. It's so messy. It's everywhere and ruining my studio. It gets everywhere and on everything, but you still have to do it.

 T: I'm really interested in your drawing practice. In my experience, drawing is one of those things that you did as an undergraduate, and the "real stuff" is when you get into your sculpture or painting classes. Why did you stick to drawing as a basis for your work?

H: There was a time when I abandoned it–graduate school will do that to you. There's a lot of reasons why I choose drawing. I try to be considerate about when I use it–and I mean traditional drawing, like medium on paper. Part of me is just indulgent. I love drawing because it's immediate. I used to be a dancer, and I think there's something about it and how I think and make drawings that relate to the body. I'm not making figurative work, although I think I'm moving back in that direction, and that's really scary. Painting is so labored. I love painting, but I don't make them anymore. I don't have the time and energy.

T: Something else I'm curious to hear more about is your content. There seems to be this imaginative, dreamlike quality to them. How do you come up with your imagery?

H: It ranges from project to project. I have this idea of the collective conscience, of appropriating imagery from the internet. Gleaning and stealing from everyday people is really interesting, and related well to the subject matter that I'm doing. Right now I'm doing these police brutality things, but before that I've been doing work about natural disasters. In a way, it's voyeuristic because you're using images that people have posted online of their tragedies. It sounds so corrupt. But I'm taking those, and recontexualizing them based on my own memories. I'm using the idea of collecting images that don't belong to me, but constructing images that feel real to me.

J: There's a series you did where you specifically talk about your house burning down when you were 15 and how that affected the content you're using. When did this start manifesting itself in your work? Was it a conscience decision?

H: I started working with themes related to disasters in 2011, but I didn't consciously decide to make work about my personal experiences, at least not at first. In fact, I really thought I was doing something interesting, something more universal. My sister sent me these photographs I took when I was 15 of our burnt house and my stuff in piles. I realized then that I was making these images that look exactly like this thing that happened to me as a teenager. I was drawing imagery from this but wasn't even thinking about it. It was kind of ridiculous. I have these themes that I've been interested in that are obviously related to childhood memories. I thought, "oh, I'm making all this work about the aftermath of storms and natural disasters" which has expanded into all these other things, but essentially I was just making work about my childhood.

T: Do you feel like when you had that "ah-ha" moment, that was your unconscious playing itself out on paper?

H: Yeah, I think all of us are making autobiographical work, even conceptual artists, or those trying to get as minimal as possible, I still feel like what we are doing is portraiture. There's no way that you can separate yourself - your intentions, experience, ideas - from your work. It's problematic and I feel like anything can go at this point. I do think of all my work as self-portraiture.

T: I want to talk more about your idea of disaster. You've been working in a series related to disaster for awhile. What has kept the momentum going for dealing with disaster?

H: I think that source material is endless. I really do have an apocalyptic view of the world-politics, the environment. It's non-stop fodder to fuel my obsession with disaster. It's everywhere. In a way, I would like to break out of it, but I'm surrounded by it all day. Maybe I'm pessimistic, but I think that I'm actually kinda of a pleasant person. I'm kinda happy. It's just that it reflects the world that I think we live in, which is kind of sad.

J: You're capturing these moments before or after a disaster. While there is tension and chaos, the images are still beautiful and constrained. Even the border you choose on your works are very crisp-I don't know how you keep your paper clean when you're using charcoal. Could you talk about how those themes of chaos and beauty tie into your work?

H: I think that it is the trickery of my work. I don't mean that I'm trying to trick the viewer, but I'm authentically trying to make beautiful things out of these dark topics. I feel that in some ways beauty is subversive. Sentimentality is subversive. It's so bad and something you don't do in the art world. I'm interested in those things and try to use them to my benefit to pull the viewer in. I think that my work is very reflective of my life.

It is chaos, but completely structured and formed. It is like the little chaos globes that are neatly packed together.

J: As an artist and professor, how do you manage your time?

H: It's really been hard for me. My career was really focused on getting a real job and getting tenure. I've been doing all these professional things. I've had an agenda, and I've got a great job. I love it. I'm chair of my department and have all these crazy responsibilities. It really makes it difficult to make work because there's no time. When I'm working in the studio, it's really limited. It's like maybe one or two evenings a week, mostly on the weekend. Sometimes I don't even go to the studio besides once a month. It's really brutal. I'll do most of my work during spring break or Christmas holiday. I do really have to time manage because I do have a rigorous exhibition schedule that I have to stay on top of. I'm really tired. I think I'm organized, but my husband would say that I'm crazy disorganized. It's all perspective, but you have to have some level of organization to keep the schedule going.

T: I think when you decide to be an artist you immediately make your life chaotic and you have to find some structure to keep the pieces together. On another note, I see your works as being individual, but working well together as an installation. Would you agree with that or do you see your exhibitions as one piece together?

H: I think that I'm creating bodies of work and not so much individual pieces. It's difficult for me to consider the picture plane. I often don't think about my drawings as single pieces. They're really these moments connected to this other work and the installations are like that as well. Often, the installations are in context with drawings or other works. I don't know how I feel about it. I think that the installations are not even as strong as the drawings - I don't know even if they could live on their own. It's a weird thing.

J: I find your installations are often whimsical while your drawings have this tone of being serious. Is that intentional?

H: I really do like the playfulness of the sculptures. Again, I think of them as drawings, but in the physical space. For me, they are theatrical. It's one of my faux pas in the art world. I'm doing all of them. It's a way to physically engage with the viewer on a difficult level and it's very appealing for those who see it. I love them because they're physical things that I can work through. They're whimsical and have an element of fantasy.

T: From 2011 with Beautiful Monsters to your most recent installation titled, Domestic Brutality at grayDUCK, there is a fantastical element to your work.

H: Yeah, I'm interested in the fallibility of memory which then leads to this idea that truth is constructed and facts are arbitrary. All of our knowledge and language is subjective and there's no real truth in anything. It's interesting to find the truth in something, and some fantasy can be more truthful than reality which is interesting to me.

J: What artists have - both contemporary and non-living - have inspired your work?

H: I have a huge list of artists that I love. I know that I'm influenced by all of them, but I don't consciously think about that when I'm making work. I don't look at their work in the context that I want to make work like that or even understand how they made it. My major top loves are Anselm Kiefer and Eric Fischl who was doing some amazing bad painting and now he's doing some amazing great painting. Kiefer is so visceral and tactile. There's physicality in the work and embedded darkness. I love Kara Walker, and again, it's this theatricality and social content. I'm trying to think of some dead artists, but it's kind of hard. Honestly, the Van Gogh drawings of the fields. It's almost like they've been rediscovered over the past 50 years because they're all over the

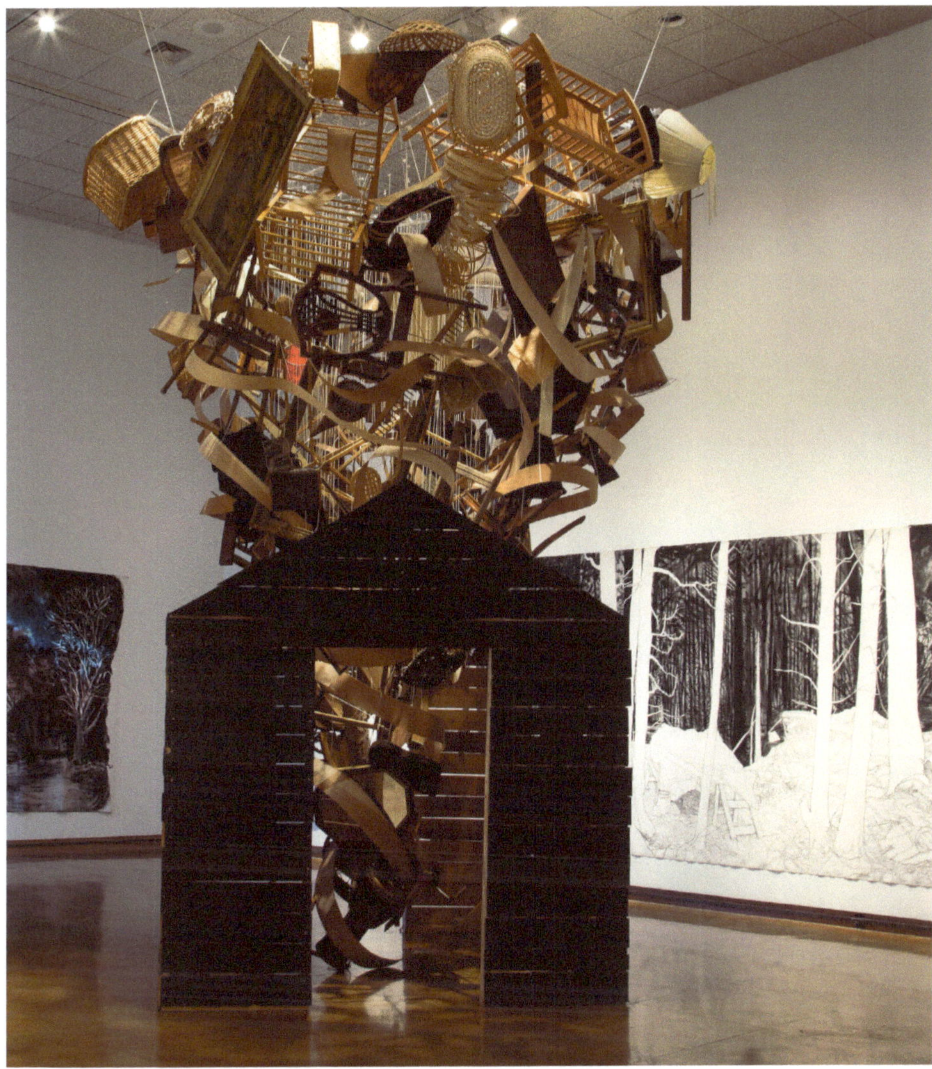

internet. They're the most amazing drawings I've ever seen. I'm obsessed with mark making, and I think about it like I do line. It has as much significance.

J: A lot of your old work deals with environmental disaster, but your two newest works are navigating towards human disasters, which are experiences in culture. Could you tell us more about that?

H: I'm really excited and terrified of my new work because as artists, we are often skirting around the topic. We make work that insinuates things, but not any specifics. We create feelings, but not doing political work directly. I've been doing that for a long time. Often I'll start with something that is very specific, but then I will quickly make it general and I'll regurgitate it until it gets out of my system. I don't feel that it's the most appropriate technique for this new work that I'm making. I'm a very political person, but I haven't made very political work. I think my politics have been subtle in the work, but I think there's potential for the work to be much more politically driven and take a stand on something. A lot of artists stop before we get there because we want to pose questions without being accountable for our critique. It's mostly a critique of myself, and I'm also very careful about the content since I'm a white, middle class professor, and a liberal. I was raised a poor country girl, but I'm trying to talk about issues that aren't affecting me directly, but that are important to me like police brutality. I can't not make work about it.

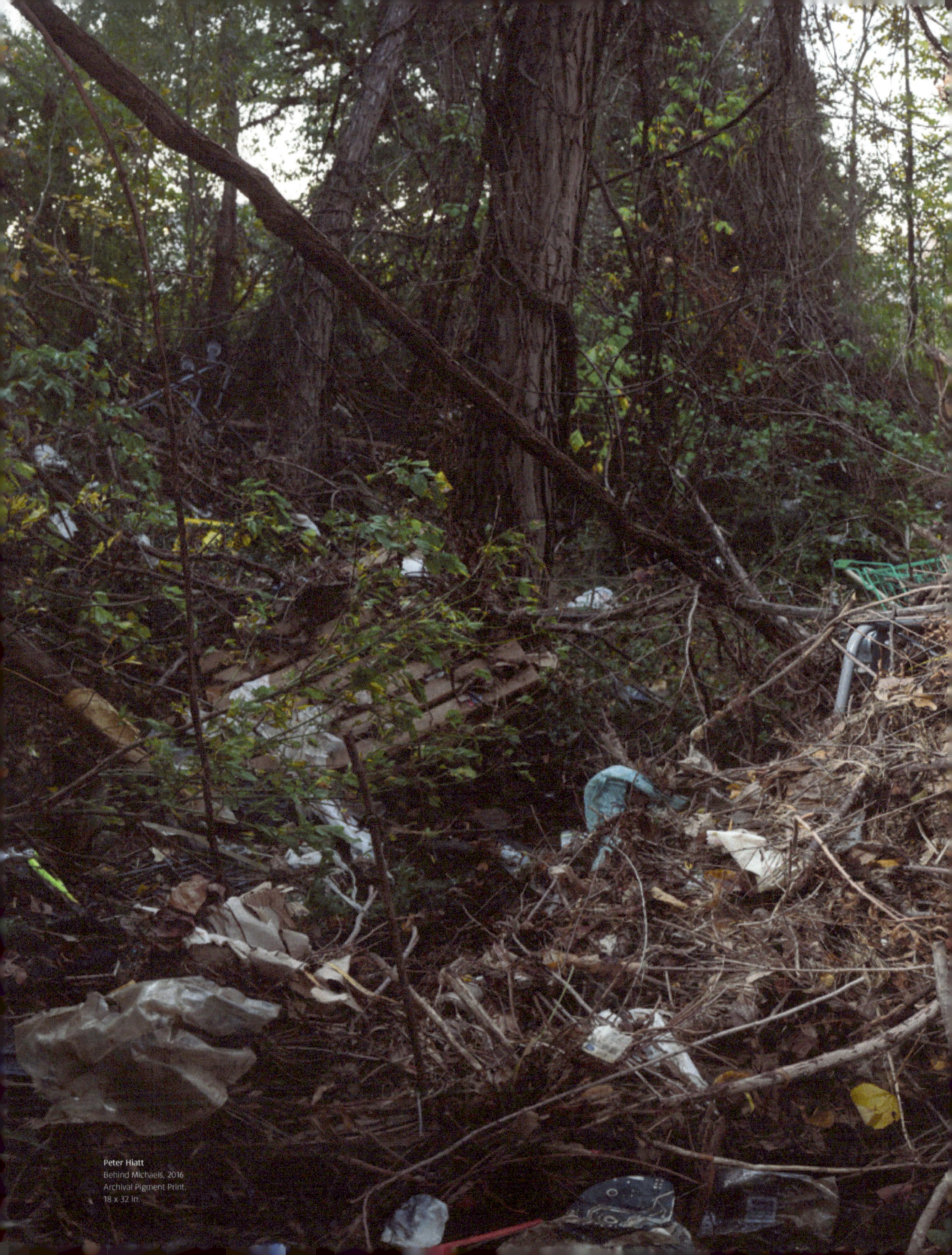

Peter Hiatt
Behind Michaels, 2016
Archival Pigment Print,
18 x 32 in.

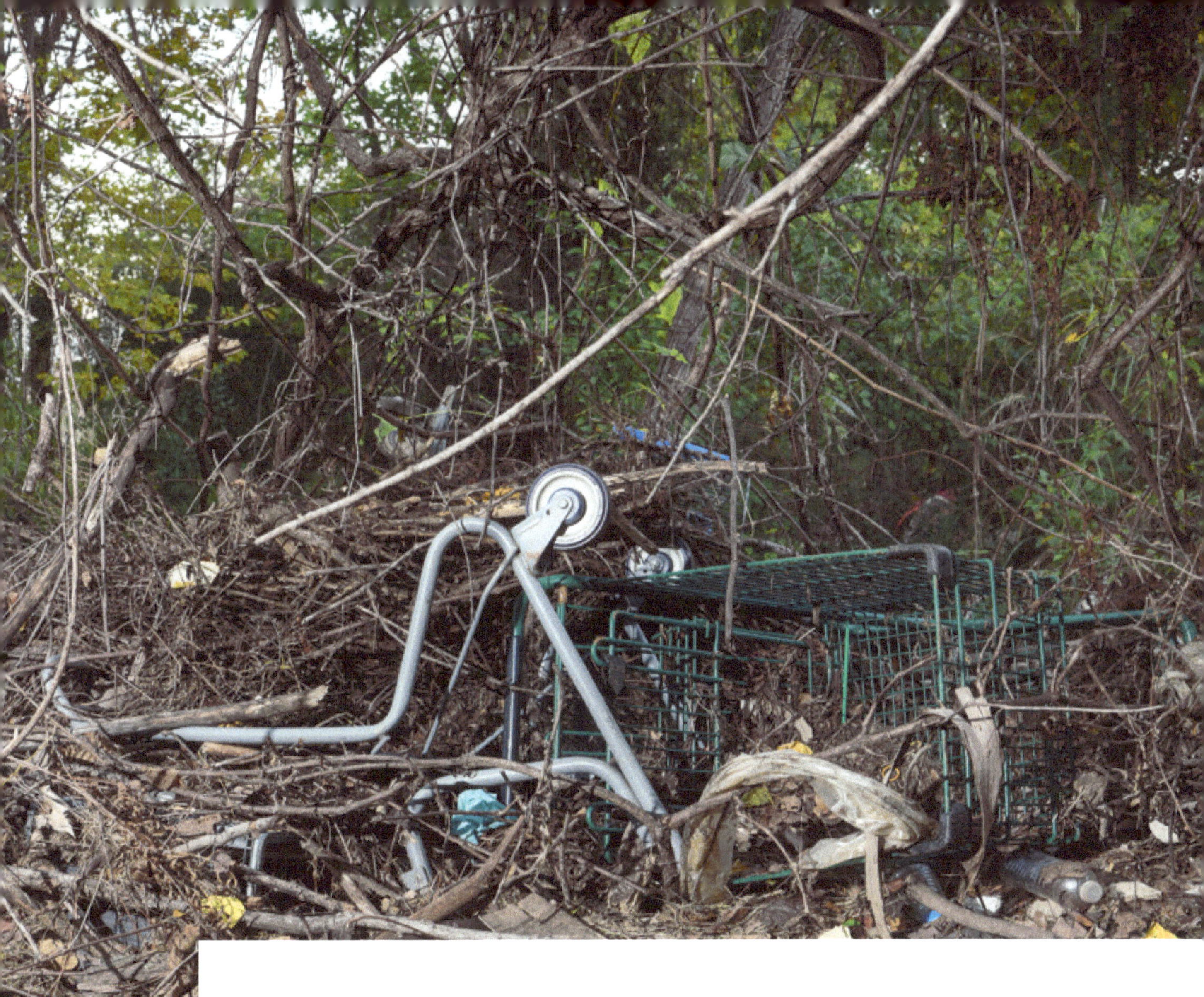

An interview with Peter Hiatt

No Unsacred Places

Works by Peter Hiatt
Interviewed by Dannie Liebergot

D: You received both your BFA (2012) and MFA (2017) in photography. How did you become interested in the medium and who are some your influences?

P: I first discovered photography as an art form when I made and submitted work for a 4-H competition. Something about the medium, especially black and white, silver gelatin photography, which was what I first used, had a way of isolating and emphasizing the sublime elements of the world. I find it to be the most effective tool for me to express myself and my ideas to the world.

D: In your project No Unsacred Places, your images appear to be of nature but quickly draw attention to the garbage that is embedded within the landscape creating a combination of beauty and unsightly consequences of rapid consumerism. How and when did you become aware of these places?

P: In my series No Unsacred Places, I photographed the backs of strip malls. I was attracted by how these places existed as objects. They have a certain monolithic beauty when viewed from behind, where there is no signage visible, and no people or cars around them. As I photographed them, I began to think about how they existed within the social contract. These strip malls are ubiquitous in America; they are so common that people rarely think about the implications of their existence. They are places of movement, designed for people to move through. They are an example of what Marc Augé calls "Non-Places" in his book of the same name. I began to become more aware of the designation of human movement, and how that was communicated in a strip mall, and in the larger retail park. There are clear designated entry and exit points to these stores, and aisles of movement within them. Just as there are designations for the movement of people, there are designations for the movement of automobiles. There are symbols and lines that indicate paths of movement, and where to park. There are also subtler cues; things that imply directions of movement without being explicit. Behind the strip malls there were often thickly wooded ditches, in which the vegetation grew so dense that one could not see into them. These places serve to designate the edge of the retail park, creating the clear implication that this barrier is not to be breached by humans. I decided to break the social contract of the retail park, and enter into these places.

D: You refer to "intellectual invisibility" in your statement; can you elaborate on how this idea becomes central in this body of work and where it comes from?

P: Many powerful institutions use this phenomenon to preserve power. They escape scrutiny because they are thought to be an intrinsic part of the world. An example of this phenomenon, which I explored in a previous project, is golf. It is an accepted part of society, and most people either participate in the sport or know people who do. However, it quickly becomes absurd when presented as an abstract concept. It proposes that you drastically reshape the land of an area and go to enormous expense to grow and maintain non-native grasses on that land to conform to an ideal of the landscape that originated in Britain, all to play a game that simply entails hitting a tiny ball with a club. It is an absurd notion, but it is rarely questioned, because golf has existed long enough, and is ubiquitous enough to escape scrutiny. The idea of intellectual invisibility applies to the drainage ditches as well. Retail centers have become ubiquitous. Most Americans alive today have grown up with these institutions in their community. They do not consider the implications of the retail centers, or the drainage ditches that border them. The drainage ditches add another layer of camouflage, because their dense foliage literally hides them from view. The strip malls exist in plain site; what makes the drainage ditches interesting is that they can be breached, and inside them one can see the true nature of things. Inside the ditches is a messy struggle between our society's abusive, unsustainable relationship with nature, and the capacity of nature to adapt and absorb all of our refuse into itself.

D: What does your process look like when you search for these places and how do you go about photographing them?

P: My process starts on Google Maps. I use the satellite view to find locations that look promising. I look for medium-to-large retail centers that have a creek or wooded area bordering them. Later, I will go to scout the locations that I have tagged.

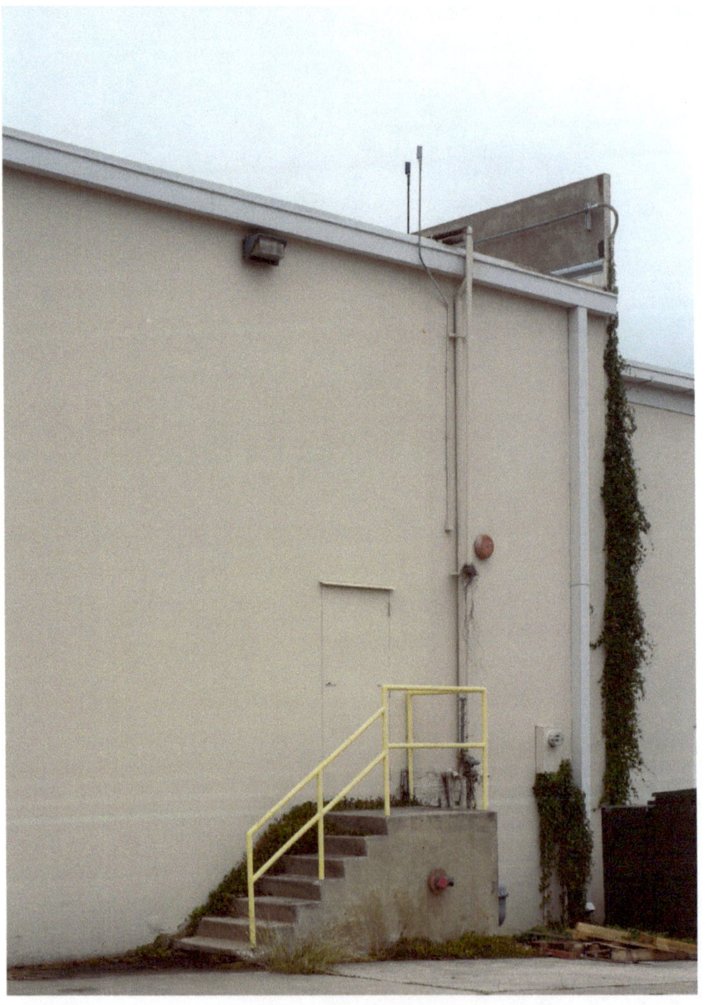

When I check the location, I make a note of whether or not it is worth photographing. I then go back to the good locations to photograph, one at a time. I have taken to wearing coveralls, boots, and gloves, after I suffered a severe reaction to poison ivy. Because the ditches are so dark relative to the sky, I can only photograph at dawn, dusk, or on a cloudy day. Cloudy days are extremely valuable, because they allow me the most time, and they are rare in Texas. Each photograph is a panorama made up of many separate photographs. This method has many advantages, but it means that each image takes a long time to make. I usually am only able to make one or two images per visit. I often use the panorama feature on my phone in order to get a preview of what the finished image will look like. Because I cannot look through the viewfinder at a preview of the finished piece, I have had to gain an intuitive sense of what the final image will look like. I have gotten better at this over time, but it is still a challenge.

D: Do you use film or digital photography?

P: I currently use exclusively digital photography. I have a deep love and appreciation of film photography, but practical considerations have kept me away from it since graduating from Texas Tech. I worked in film about half the time while I was there and had a lab. After I graduated and was on my own, my process shifted to entirely digital, which was much more practical without access to a wet lab. As time has gone by, I have also exploited other aspects of digital photography beyond its economical advantages. Digital photography allows me to take forty photographs and seamlessly combine them into one huge panorama. Digital printing allows me to make 42" wide images economically. I am not immune to the beauty and elegance of film, and I appreciate the more tactile process, but those benefits are outweighed by the economy and imaging potential of digital processes.

D: These are mostly large-scale prints; how do you achieve that scale?

P: When planning my exhibition, I struggled with the scale of the prints. I wanted to make huge prints on beautiful paper, with archival framing and mounting. However, this was not economically feasible. I eventually decided to make the work in two sizes: medium-sized framed prints on beautiful paper, and huge prints made on adhesive fabric that stick directly to the wall. The fact that I capture the images as panoramas made up of many photographs gave the images sufficient resolution to allow them to be enlarged to huge proportions while still being sharp. I printed on the adhesive fabric myself, and tiled several pieces to create 7.5 feet by 14 feet installations. I love the huge, immersive size, and the adhesive fabric, while not as good-looking as photo paper, yields surprisingly crisp and vibrant images.

D: Photography is quite an expensive medium for art. If you didn't have a budget for printing and installation, would this change your presentation of this work?

P: If I did not have a budget for printing and installation, my first impulse would be to make huge, beautiful prints. I would print at least 40" on the short end, on Hahnemuhl Photo Rag Satin, then have them mounted on Dipbond and framed under museum glass. I would also be interested in making huge installations of prints adhered directly to the wall. I would find a big place to mount an exhibition, then have walls built to my specifications for each print. I would build circular rooms, with a single print adhered to the entire wall, so that it completely surrounds the viewer. I would also play with ambient sound installation to add to the experience. With unlimited resources, my main ambition would be to make truly immersive exhibitions. I love the work of James Turrell in that respect, and I think it would be amazing to emulate the immersiveness of his installations in a photography-based exhibition.

D: How has the transition out of graduate school been for you? Any art collectives or groups that you are a part of?

P: I have not been out of graduate school for long, so I do not have a good perception of the complete transition out of it. Mostly I have been concentrating on finding work and bringing about some stability to my life. I have not yet joined any artist organizations. When I have my working life a little more settled, I would like to look into joining a coop or organization. I like the idea of having more impetus for making work in a timely manner, now that the pressure from school is gone. I would also appreciate the community of peers that such a group would offer.

D: Do you have any projects that you are currently working on?

P: I am currently working on a series of photographs of skate parks. I am interested in the lengths people go to recreate natural phenomena in an urban setting. Skateboarding began as an urban simulation of surfing, and the curved structures of skate parks are recreations of waves. Other aspects of skate parks actually recreate artificial structures, like stairs and hand rails. I find the psychology behind these places fascinating, and I enjoy the process of aestheticizing them photographically.

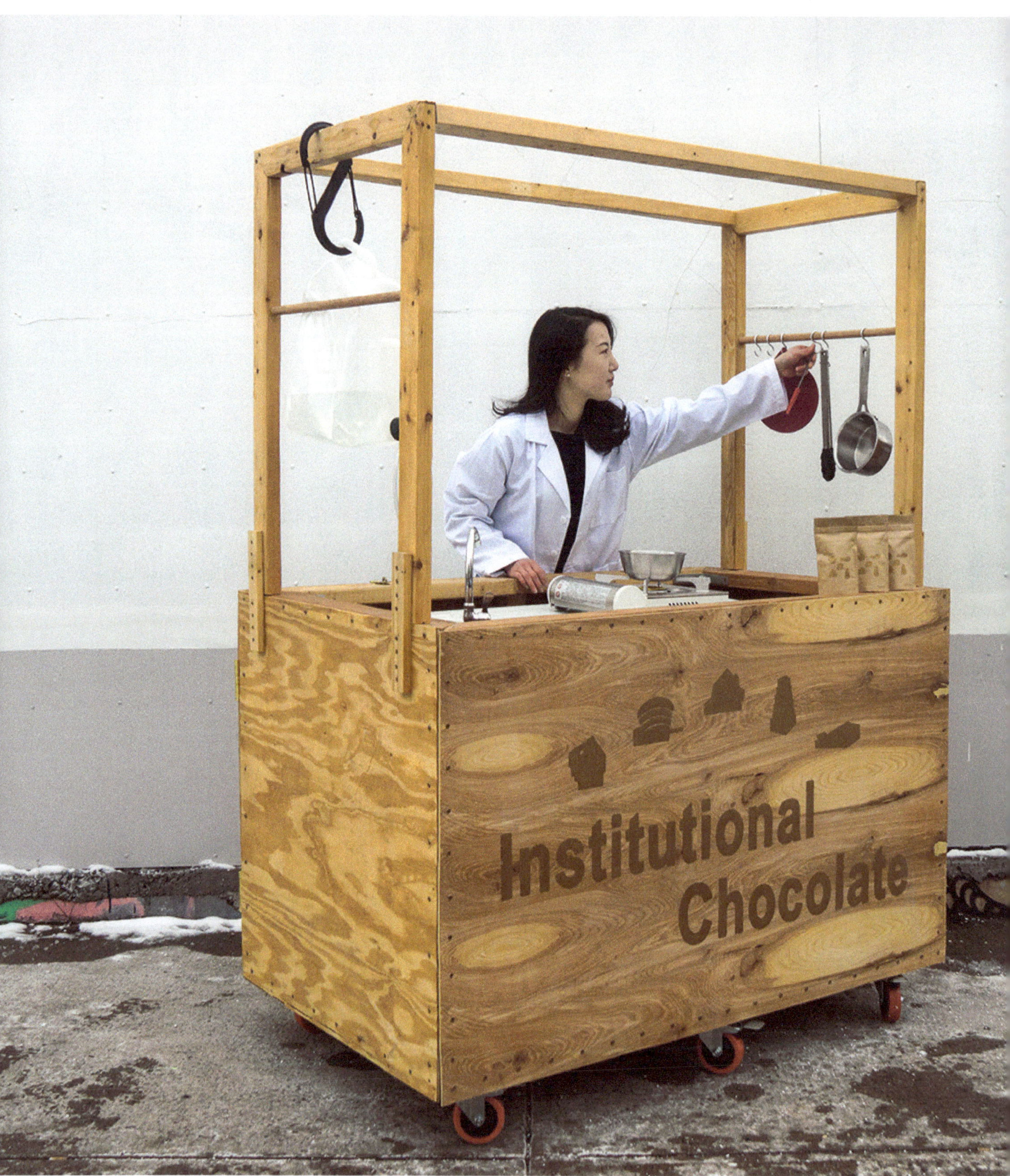

Institutional
Chocolate

Bonam Kim
Mobile Kitchen, 2017
Wood, wheel, paint, table,
kitchen ware,
33 x 55 x 75 in.

Engaging the Audience Through Performance

An interview with Bonam Kim

Works by Bonam Kim

Interviewed by Ty Bishop

T: In your artist statement, you state that "I cannot escape the need for psychological dependency, nostalgic desires and memories that seem to guarantee security and comfort. I'm curious, how does this play out in your performance piece Mobile Kitchen – Institutional Chocolate?

B: It's a hard question. Most of the works that I made in the last two years have been focusing on the feelings of nostalgia, displacement and struggle that come with cultural identity since moving from Seoul to New York. However, recently I've been interested in making work about issues that people usually take for granted or easily ignore. I believe that this is one of the good things that artists do in this society. I can say that the Mobile Kitchen is the piece that is in a transition period and that broadens the scope of my work.

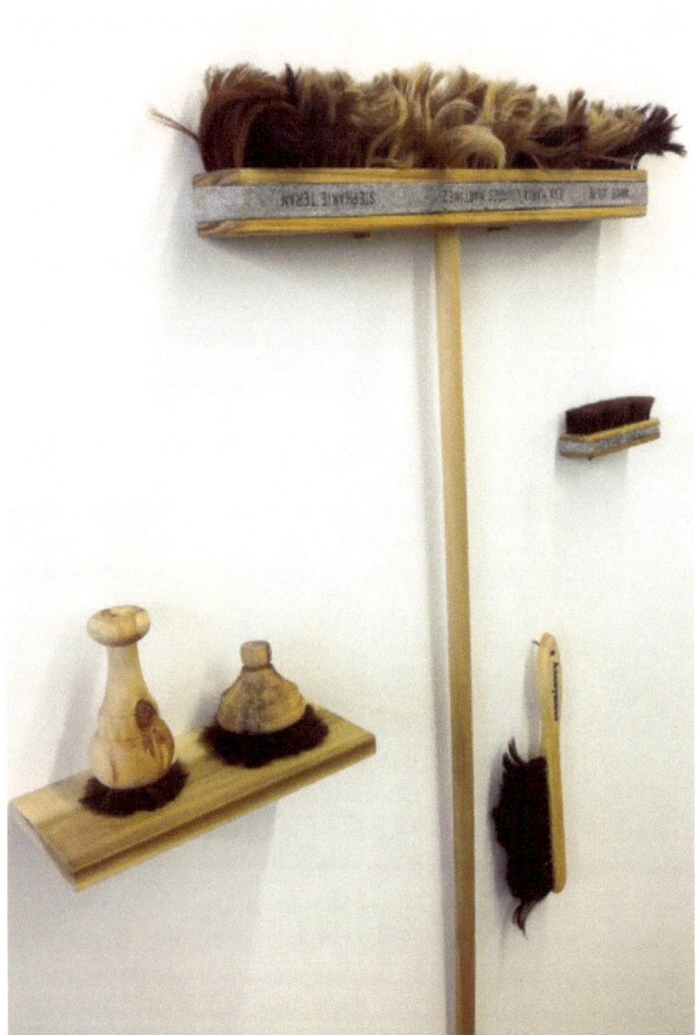

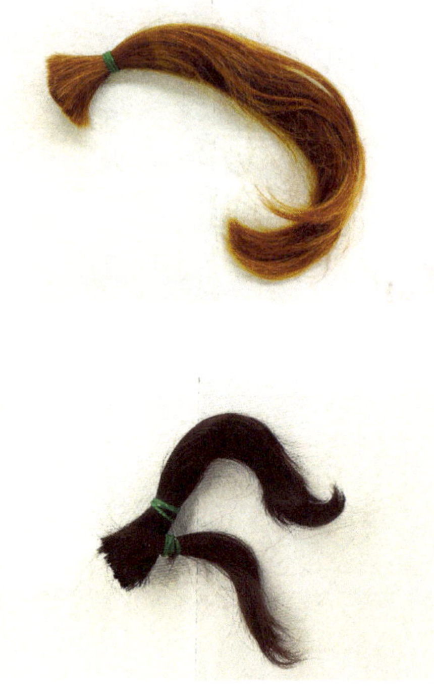

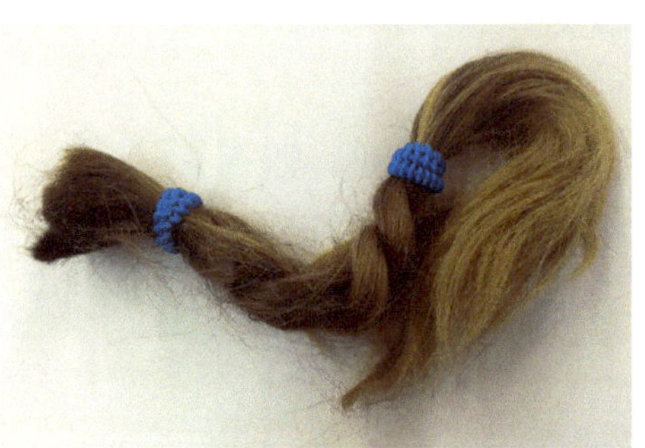

T: Mobile Kitchen – Institutional Chocolate seems so pleasant–even your facial expression in the photo elicits a kind of child-like joy. However, it's also clear that you're making a statement about the art world since the Guggenheim and MOMA PS1 are two of the buildings you chose to make chocolate silhouettes out of. Can you talk about why you chose those buildings in particular?

B: I always feel that there is an invisible wall between an artwork and the viewer whenever I go to the museum. In an effort to express my feeling, I chose the five museums that I most often visit in New York, where I live.

T: Why was white chocolate important for this piece?

B: Because the white chocolate shows how I see the museum in terms of color, the white cube, for example, or representing a kind of hallmark. Also, the white chocolates melt away like a mirage, as do my sweet desires. This reveals my skeptical attitude towards the systems and institutions that regulate art.

T: You've completed several art degrees in sculpture, and you recently graduated with an MFA from Pratt. In your earlier work, your pieces were mostly attached to the wall. Now it's clear that you're interested in performance. Why did you make the switch?

B: Moving from Seoul and leaving familiar scenes behind and moving to a place that is so different in so many ways, was an opportunity for me to let go

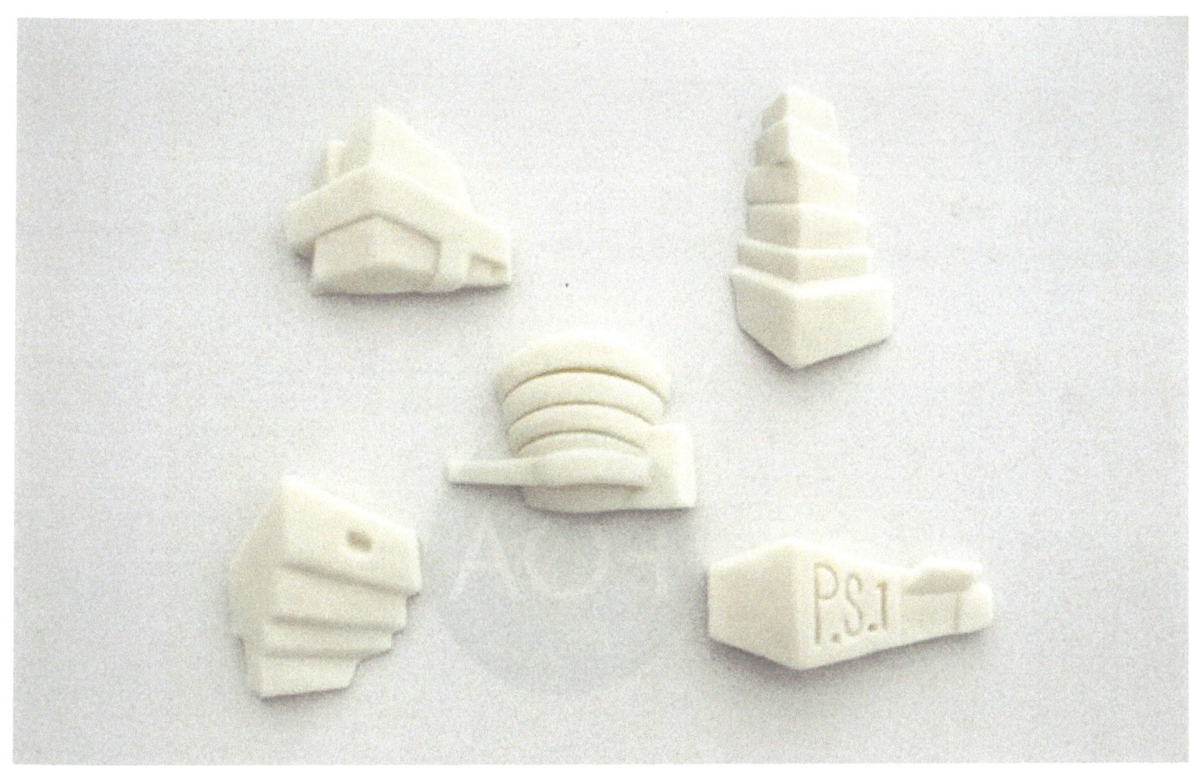

of the concepts that I had accumulated in the past, and it has both excited and scared me. Being part of a particular culture and adjusting to a new culture are a kind of performance. In New York, where various cultures and ethnic groups coexist, I have gone through many changes in terms of thoughts and perspectives, and unexpectedly encountered other people and experienced things have been provocative and interesting. As I think about my recent work Through the Crack, Broom Project, and Institutional Chocolate, I want my sculpture to act as a tool or device and I like the experience of engaging with the public.

T: Another project that you submitted was Broom Project. I must say, it totally caught me off guard when I realized that the broom was constructed of human hair. Was this your intention? Whose hair did you use?

B: Yes, it's my intention. I place ads on Craigslist asking for people to cut their hair and send me the clippings. Some friends who know about my project also saved their hair for me. It's an ongoing project and I try to keep making more brooms and brushes. Let me know if you have plans to cut your hair (hahaha). You can also participate in my project.

T: What I love about this piece is that it's relatively simple -a wooden stick, human hair, and resin, yet it communicates something complex. Can you talk about what you drove you to make this piece?

B: I think hair is one of the richest resources of the self. Hair is relevant to every human being; we grow it, cut it, style it, and depilate, and sometimes it fails to grow at all. Yet even as we manipulate and exert our preferences on it, hair maintains a complex and enigmatic function in our lives. Acting as a marker of identity, it has remained paramount throughout history in cultures across the world. Eventually I intend to use the brushes and brooms with human hair to clean neglected areas of New York, effectively performing a collaborative, civic gesture where the people are involved in cleaning their city.